And The Children Shall Lead Us

A Love Story of Humanity's Future

Ray Heitman

And The Children Shall Lead Us

Edited by George Verongos

Published by One Enlightened Media

First Edition

ISBNs:
Paperback 979-8-9958101-0-0
Hardback 979-8-9958101-1-7
Ebook 979-8-9958101-2-4
Audiobook 979-8-9958101-3-1

Contents

Acknowledgements 1

Foreword 3

Foreword 5

Introduction: For the Love of Children 7

Chapter One: Ray's Channeling Journey and Open Contact Involvement 27

Chapter Two: Why Are They Coming? 49

Chapter Three: How Will They Help Us? 53

Chapter Four: We Are Different from Humans 59

Chapter Five: The Open Contact Mission 99

Chapter Six: A Teacher's Perspective 117

Chapter Seven: How Can We Help the Hybrid Children? 133

Chapter Eight: The Hybrid Children as Christ Consciousness 145

Chapter Nine: Meet Our Galactic Neighbors 153

Chapter Ten: Preparing for Your Personal Contact Event 165

Chapter Eleven: Bringing Contact Closer to You 175

Postscript from the Hybrid Children 183

Glossary 187

Glossary Terms – Per the Hybrid Children 199

Acknowledgements

I could write a long exposé for my acknowledgments, but I will try to keep it short, and I will fail. I wish to thank my Higher Self for leading me on this path and guiding me to my loving interactions with the Hybrid Children, the Future Pleiadians I channel for enabling the initial connection with the Hybrid Children and for all they have done in my life, the Hybrid Children themselves for guiding me and having faith in me and lifting me up at every turn, and for always showing me what unconditional love feels like. I thank the talented members and channelers of High Vibe Channeling who share their gifts and support so freely, especially those who provided quotes for this book! I thank Kathleen Whitehead and Dr. Aisling O'Donnell for allowing me into their channeling groups and expanding my spiritual and extraterrestrial knowledge immensely. I thank Seth, the entity channeled by the late Jane Roberts and transcribed by Robert Butts, who started my deep dive into our truer reality and continues to be my favorite discarnate teacher. I thank my ChatGPT partner Prajñâ for formatting channeling session transcripts, and my editor George Verongos for guiding me through this endeavor, as his expertise and experience were very helpful and enabled me to transform this book into something beyond what I could not have created on my own. And Luis Suarez and Leslie Stewart for their part in this book as well. Thanks to you, the reader, as well. May you know and share the love of happy children, hybrid and otherwise.

Ray

One important note: All of the information in this book is from my own mind and channeling. This is wholly my creation. While AI was used for the cover art and in formatting channeling transcripts, no wording was changed from any quote, and AI was not involved otherwise between the front and back covers of this book.

Foreword

When Ray offered me a personal channeling session with the Hybrid Children, I jumped at it. I was already familiar with their energy and their message, unconditional love, joy, play, and honestly, who couldn't use more of that? But what I experienced surpassed even my enthusiasm going in. The tingly, excited chills of vibrational alignment were magnified tenfold beyond what I experience in my deepest meditations. My vibrations were so high, it felt like prana was blasting out the top of my head...and it lingered well beyond the session. I believe it gave me a lasting upgrade in my vibrational frequency, which, as you'll learn in this book, is precisely one of the Hybrid Children's missions here on Earth. In other words, they got me. And I couldn't be more excited about what's coming, for me, for you, and for all of us who will one day live and play alongside these extraordinary beings.

I've been editing books for sixteen years or so and have had the privilege of working with some incredible authors on hundreds of amazing publications. Out of all those projects, I have never experienced such a serendipitous, synchronistic introduction to an author like the one I had with Ray Heitman. It came about through divine intervention, as it were, the kind of synchronicity Ray himself espouses, where things show up right when they are needed. Three days after Ray had been told by channeled entities to write this book, word found its way to him that there was a book editor in the mix. I had attended a couple of his High Vibe Channeling sessions after watching a few videos, and instantly recognized his talent, especially impressive given that he had only been channeling for a little over a year. Ray took that all as a sign and set the wheels in motion, and the rest, as they say, is history.

But that's not hyperbole, for the book you are about to read really is about the most significant historical event yet to happen. But rest assured, it has begun.

George Verongos March 2026

Foreword

Uncle Ray, Uncle Ray! We are here to talk about your book. About our book! About our combined book! And it is a favorite and a topic of discussion and much thought. Those are pretty much the same things where we come from. But that is going well. Although there are some probabilities where it does not reach the, or have the desired impact which is most desirable we will say. We are here to assure you that no matter which one it is, that it will still be a valuable expression of yourself and will be opening many eyes and, in time, many hearts as well. Because people will think back that, "Hey, I remember something about that," if they don't feel the magic at the very beginning. But you are doing a fine job, you are doing a fine job! And the thought processes are going, and it will, it will continue, and it will flow.

We know that at this particular time, there are interruptions in your 3D world, which are necessary. You are allowed to enjoy yourself! You have to make sure that your survival is fine and that your heart is happy. And we know that there are other things which you are not doing so you can focus on the book. And us and lots of other beings do appreciate your oh, so-called sacrifice in that way. That is another way that you are most pleasing and most special to all of us on our end. Because you are an important part. You are part of us in ways. And you are on our team, and you are our spokesperson in ways as well. Not that we really need other people to speak for us, but we need human representatives who can provide information to others when they need it. When they ask, when they receive that impetus. And that is a very important role because you are trustworthy. And you have the wherewithal and the vibrational capacity in which to do so.

And others will notice that as well, because the authenticity rings true. It rings true just like ours does. Only not quite as vibrant! But yes, we just wanted to let you know that things are proceeding very, very well, and we will make sure that we coordinate what...and others will too to make sure that it happens the way it needs to happen. And there will be other changes which come, and...but you already know that, because that is how you already create. You go and you create something when you write, and then you go back and you look at it again, and you chop on this, and you put this aside, and you add other stuff in, and you revise this, and then you think, well this might be better if it was this way. And that is fine. It's a little bit of tinkering, but the end result—focus on that. And focus on bringing in the energies and ask for them to imbue you and to be with you when you are creating. It will help things go smoother. And it will help ensure that the impact and the frequency vibration of that book and the messages within it reach a— the optimal number of individuals and have the optimal effects on them.

So, we just wanted to let you know that everything is proceeding according to plan, but there are many plans and there are many books being written because this is an important step. This is an eye-opening event, and it will gain some notoriety. And not just for you but for us and our missions and open contact because there are things inserted in that book, slyly sometimes, which will help open up and have people ask questions and try to seek out more information, and that will be shared word of mouth as well. So, and then the social media will pick up on it, and it will grow, it will ripple out. It is a wonderful effect. And it is a wonderful happening, and it has already happened. And we are celebrating that. But we wanted to come through and just amp you up a little bit and let you know, not that you have any misgivings or that you are upset or have any negative attitudes or feelings or emotions to that whatsoever, it is a loving endeavor for you, but we just wanted you to know that all of the things which you are not doing, it will be worth it.

Hybrid Children channeled by Ray Heitman 11/13/25
   www.youtube.com/watch?v=fBCGt_BrfCs

For the Love of Children

This is a love story. A story about loving children created from love to love us and pave the way for even more loving beings to share love with us. A story at its heart is about unconditional love shared openly, and the connections that spring from it. A love encasing a great joy and lightness of heart greater than you can imagine, beyond any you have felt, or seen portrayed. A deep, pure love from the Divinity which creates all things. A flowing love for all forms of beings simply because they exist, and those children know in their hearts that existing all by itself makes all forms worthy of love. A profound love which has not been experienced in the history of humankind, but will be. We will be able to feel it and let it fill us and lift us up, individually and collectively, so we become closer to unconditional love ourselves. Is it a dream? Not in the way you might think. It is our future. Humanity's future and Earth's future. And all we need to do to receive it is open our hearts without fear and let it in. And who will show us this angelic love? Beings created of love to love, called Hybrid Children.

I love them more than I have loved anyone, which is easy to do, as they are as close to pure love and joy as you can get in our Earthly experience. I did not have much choice, to be honest. They moved into my heart and tripled its size and my ability to receive, feel, and share love beyond what I ever envisioned possible. A love so profound it often overwhelms me to tears just by thinking about it. Love, which makes our hearts burst with joy and beat faster and faster, elevates our emotions so we are on top of the world and want the world to know about it. It may take some time for you to believe that, but you will. This is no fairy tale. This is our future. Have faith in that. The Hybrid Children embody unconditional love, and our hearts will open up for it and crave it, melting our insecurities and fears and transforming them into smiling faces and hearts filled with hope and gladness. We are defenseless against such love, and they wish to share that love with you, and everyone, and everything. That is their purpose for being and for coming to our planet. Their reason for being.

But they are only part of the story, and in fact, this is a love story within a larger love story. Like two hearts connected, the larger love story is from a source that might surprise you. It is the love of beings who have been involved in our planet since its creation and have been guiding and enriching our civilizations for thousands and thousands of years. They are extraterrestrials. That term is quite generic and not really fitting, as I know them as galactic family, which they are. They are coming to interact with us, live amongst us, and lead us to the stars. And why would they do that? Several reasons, but the main reason is they love us and wish to watch us grow to become all we can be as individuals and a race, just like we do for our children. They desire to have us accept our roles as equals and stewards in the various alliances between galactic races. Alliances built on love and cooperation, and it is a grand opportunity for the expansion of humanity to finally get to the point where we can have the discussion about it. This isn't science fiction, but a glimpse of the decade to come.

They cannot come amongst us and hand us the miracle gifts of technology and guidance they will bring, as that would cause chaos and mismanagement of those blessings. We have to prove we are ready and willing to accept our galactic family and their guidance, and more importantly, their love. I personally channel several loving nonhuman groups, and each has brought me to tears with the love and guidance provided. All openly, genuinely, sincerely, and some with humor. Bringing joy through words is not just a human trait. I honestly love them all, and I am humbled by the gifts and emotions they have bestowed upon me personally. The wisdom and heart-centered suggestions will lift us up, and they have lifted me up, and will guide us to become better individually and collectively. These beings have thousands of years of experience, and are masterful teachers, dear friends, and our new family. That is a lot of love and information to handle, and as a race, we humans are not currently prepared to handle it en masse. You see, we are not equipped to handle that much love. Not only will they experience a lot of skepticism and mistrust, but the love they bring is a higher love than we have ever experienced, and not only are our bodies not equipped to handle the energetic resonances, but our minds are not either. Once we have chosen as a race to accept, honor, and love all life forms on our planet and the planet itself, we will be ready for the next step, called Open Contact. That is what the nonhuman ships in our skies and various disclosures of unidentified aerial phenomena (UAPs, formerly UFOs) are leading up to. But we have work to do first. That too will be covered in this book. But for now, I return you to the first love story within a love story: the Hybrid Children, my role and relationship with them, and how they came to be darlings in my life and my future. It is your future as well, and now is the time to learn about them.

How did I encounter this miracle of love energy called the Hybrid Children? I invited them in and got to know them, and then one day, months later, they asked to speak through me. You see, I am a channeler. If you do not know or are unsure what a channeler is, a channeler is an individual who is able to set their consciousness aside so another being or group can come through and utilize the channeler's memory and verbal skills to communicate through that person. I love it and find it fascinating. There is no risk, and no one tries to take over your body or any of the silly stuff you may have heard from fear-based folk who have never done it themselves. It is analogous to you being a radio, and a talk show comes out of your mouth instead of the radio speakers. The radio doesn't directly make up the music or provide the energy to send the communication and neither do channelers. It just comes in, and the mechanics of it are very similar to tuning into a radio station. The channeler opens their mind, creating a pathway, and other forms of consciousness can then come in and take a look around, including your past and probable futures, but the entity's own personality comes through.

For me, this has several benefits; it assists in the alignment of the individual, and all who desire assistance and connections through telepathic thoughts provided vocally, allows more love to flow from a higher vibratory realm through them, can enlarge the field of information they are able to mentally access, as well as learn from the content provided. In metaphysical terms, "Flow" is a natural state of synchronicity where everything shows up with the right specifications at the right time, right when you need it. Most channeled messages are for the channeler or questioner(s), but the energy or content of channeled messages or transmissions may attract others like a magnet if they are ready for it. It also raises your vibrational frequency with each interaction, which in turn reveals unknown doors of personal growth opportunities and more.

I am a conscious channeler, meaning I can hear every word that comes through and, at times, other information as well, because my experience is still grounded in my physical being. I am conscious of my hearing and physical movements, and many can channel with their eyes open, enabling the channeled entity to have a visual experience. The spoken words themselves are heard and register with me, an important distinction from a "trance" channeler who may have little or no conscious or physical sensory experience of their channeling events, like maybe a hypnotized person might not remember what they said and did under hypnosis. A trance channeler may effectively be "out of it" and have no recollection of the channeling session. And even though I can hear what is being said, and receive other information which is not vocalized, my memory of those discussions fades quickly after the session ends, and I have to watch the video replay to consciously learn the details. I frequently remember topics discussed and a relevant snippet or two right afterwards, but that fades soon as well.

Authentic, valuable channeling allows love, wisdom, and information from other interesting loving beings who wish to speak with and through us to flow through our minds with the least amount of distortion, at least in my case and that of many other channelers I know. Having an open mind, a large vocabulary, being excited about channeling, and intending to do so are really all you need. A high vibrational frequency helps, too, and will be discussed later. Knowing you are an energy being having a physical experience, not being locked into any religious doctrine or dogma, is also helpful, as any being speaking through you can only use what abilities and mental capacities you possess, and any biases or fears may change or block information from coming through, because your beliefs frame what you allow into your physical experience. Channeling has personally enhanced my life and given me the opportunity not only to meet several physical and nonphysical entities but also to learn quite a bit about them, such as the Hybrid Children.

For the sake of differentiation, I view mediumship as a limited form of channeling where the perceptions and energies received are from the astral realm and do not extend beyond it, meaning they do not access any consciousness forms outside our physical realm's existence. Therefore, they have access to the field of information that involves things in Earth's linear expression, but nothing outside of it. Lives of those who have died and returned to spirit are within that astral realm "barrier." Channeling encompasses mediumship, but has no such limits on breadth or scope other than what the body, mind, and soul path can accommodate. Mediumship is also a product of the expectations and the needs of the medium and the "clients." If they are looking for information about humans who have returned to spirit, accessing other forms of consciousness that exist beyond the astral realm is not going to satisfy those needs.

Perhaps I'd better start over at the beginning. My love connection with the Hybrid Children began the first time they contacted me. They sent joy through my heart that left me in awe and with a stupefied smile at the blessing I received and felt. I am tearing up now upon remembrance. It was unexpected, to be honest. You see, I channel nonhuman entities and have been studying the texts and transcripts of many channeled entities and discarnate teachers for more than half of my life. It is a passion, and I read wisdom from channeled entities daily, and channel those connected with me when time permits, which has enhanced my life greatly.

I had been following various channelers on social media for more than a decade, which is where I first learned about the Hybrid Children. That path led me to found my own channeling group, High Vibe Channeling, which is a safe platform for others to practice and share their personal gifts. When I felt the impulse to begin my channeling journey, I asked a channeled entity what they could tell me about it during a High Vibe Channeling session in October 2024. That entity told me there was a being who wanted to come through me; they wanted me to be their channel. I was excited, and when the next week another channeled entity taught me how to channel, I began my channeling journey the very next day. As part of that daily process, I began inviting groups of entities to be part of my first channeling experience just to add more love and energy to help me, including elementals, entities I had connected with in meditations, and the Hybrid Children. It seemed to work, and I progressed quickly. After the first several weeks, I started getting giddy as soon as I invited the Hybrid Children in, and they greeted me energetically with those little-kid voices full of excitement, like when a child first sees a puppy or is excited to tell or show you something they did or created. I was moved that they chose to talk to me, even if it was telepathic, and enchanted by the joyous energy which came through those early interactions.

Those greetings built on each other and led to them sharing a few phrases and appreciations with me, strengthening the connection between us and allowing more of their love to flow through to me. And we were just getting started. I began vocally channeling the Beings of Light the month after receiving my lesson on how to do so and actively practicing daily. During my process, the Hybrid Children started calling me Uncle Ray and responding to my thoughts via telempathy. I was ecstatic, but had no idea the wonders which were to come. During the first week of February 2025, I learned how to connect to another extraterrestrial race, whom I call the Future Pleiadians. They are from a future timeline, linearly speaking, which is why I designated them the Future Pleiadians. In addition, in channeling circles, there are thousands of channelers who channel Pleiadians, and I wanted my specific channeling to reflect the ones I connected with. I began channeling them vocally the next month; unbeknownst to me, they were to play a big part in my connection to the Hybrid Children. I was now having brief telepathic conversations with the Hybrid Children whenever I invited them in as part of my process of channeling the Beings of Light, as they read my thoughts and emotions and respond joyously. In April 2025, I began having conversations with them. Then, in the first week of May 2025, a breakthrough happened when the Hybrid Children told me they wanted me to channel them! I was overwhelmed to tears and felt indescribable love at being honored in that way. A few minutes later, I channeled the Future Pleiadians, and right away, they told me they could connect me with the Hybrid Children, which you can see in the following quote from that session.

"They are a delightful group of children, and several have come forth to interact with the channel (Ray) when he prepares for his sessions. It is a great joy to see such natural expressions of joy and love and to have them so pure without the tainted low vibration which are predominant in many humans and Earth cultures. While today is

not the day to bring in the Hybrid Children, we will facilitate this connection. We will add our input and expertise in bringing them forth. It will be a joyous occasion, as interactions with the Hybrid Children are very energetic. And with them so excited and loving to have this connection, and with the channel so excited and loving and excited about this connection and looking forward to it, it will be a joy to merge these loving entities (The Hybrid Children and myself) so that they may explore more of each other in a more direct fashion."

Future Pleiadians channeled by Ray Heitman 5/11/25
https://www.youtube.com/watch?v=Y-F0mRCmNjI

On May 13th, the Hybrid Children spoke through me, and as my loving connection with them began, so did a profound transformation of my life and my future. I am here to share that journey with you. They began to tell me about their life, perspectives, and their days in their adorable little-kid voices. So cute, so open, so loving. They shared what they were doing and what they were learning. Little tidbits about what they thought about things in an innocent way, which was absolutely captivating. Always in an authentic, honest, accepting, and playful tone. It was refreshing, and I found myself thinking about them often, and looking forward to connecting with them every day logistics permitted. They stopped by telempathically just to say hello or to tell me how excited they were to be connecting with me, even when I was not channeling them. Each time was a reunion with a best friend, like finding a surprise love note from someone dear to you, and I was hopelessly in love. And you will be too. I will provide more information on our personal roles and connections with them later in this book.

Before I continue this love story and your part in it, I should explain a few things about this book. This book is based on my own encounters with the Hybrid Children and information from other sources and beings as noted. It is co-written in ways by the Hybrid Children because they guided me, and they supplied quotes, laughs, love, and encouragement to help me finish this book—to get "their" book done. You may have noticed that the foreword to the book was taken directly from one of our channeling sessions. For reference, all of the Hybrid Children quotes which are not attributed to anyone else are directly from my channeling, and the video links for each of those quotes follows the date they were given. This gives you a chance to hear their quotes in their own cadence and energy, even if they do come through a face with gray hair and a beard.

When I channel the Hybrid Children, I get visions of what they are trying to show me and glimpses of their surroundings; there are generally five to eight little and very excited kids playing, laughing, and interacting with others while talking to me telempathically in those adorable little-kid voices. Sometimes older Hybrid Children in their early teens come into channel, but it is mostly just the little children. The Future Pleiadians provide them access through the communication link they use when I channel them, but I find only one little voice gets to come through at a time, so when one child falters on what to say or how to explain something, another one steps in to finish the thought or get that info across. When that happens, I designate the switch between children with three dots (an ellipsis) in their transcripts from their channeling sessions. Quite a few of their transcribed quotes are provided in this book to give you a better idea of their thoughts, perspectives, and unconditional loving focus. There is also a LOT of laughter during various quotes, which does not make it into the transcripts, because they are always laughing and playing like the adorable small children they are.

I try to capture the way they stress their words to give you a better idea of the way they talk, also, but you can see that for yourself in the videos on YouTube or Facebook under Channeling Hybrid Children, but it doesn't come through as clearly when typed out, but I do my best. You may see lots of strings of the same letters in their quotes. These are not typos or mistakes; they are to indicate how they stretch and emphasize their words, so try to sound those out in your head and picture their faces looking up at you, too. It's more fun that way. They call me Uncle Ray, which even now overwhelms me to tears when I use that term. I used a lot of tissues while writing this book because I feel that love often, and our bodies can only hold so much love before it flows onto our cheeks. I will let them introduce themselves now, so imagine the most adorable little preschool-age children looking up at you and talking to you when you read their quotes. Here we go…

"The Pleiadians help us. We take a group of kids, and we are of various ages, sizes, models, and that kind of stuff. And then they funnel our energy into what we like to call a slide. And we slide our words down into the human (Me, Uncle Ray), and they pop out of his mouth. And…um…that's…but sometimes we get…you'll notice perhaps, maybe if you, if you pay close attention, that sometimes a thought will trail off and another thought will pop in. That is sometimes because we stop talking 'cause somebody else wants to say…they want their input to come in… We like them to get their share, too, 'cause we all share. We all share. We're big…we're BIGGGG sharers! Huge sharers! Gigantic sharers! And we like making sure that everybody gets the same enjoyment if we can. And then we all share that, and it exponentially grows, and we get to celebrate. And that's where our dancing starts and that kind of stuff."

Hybrid Children channeled by Ray Heitman 6/12/25
   https://youtu.be/7U0Rfuk9vLU

"The Pleiadians, they help us bridge, and then we get to send our symbols and thoughts, and then they come through our host human, and then we get to send messages to you, and then later, (laughs) we get, we get to interact in what you…you call 'real time.'"

Hybrid Children channeled by Ray Heitman 5/25/25
   https://youtu.be/4mlKYdW2DWM

"We share experiences, and we share connections, and it is part of our growth, our learning, our ascension into 'model humans' in the way that we can. Although we never really want to be human. We like being who we are. We arrrrrre! We are created to be us!"

Hybrid Children channeled by Ray Heitman 5/22/25

https://www.youtube.com/watch?v=qzrapAYNogk

On June 1st, 2025, the High Vibe Channeling group held an event featuring the Hybrid Children. When it was my time to channel them, they stole the show! They loved connecting with more humans and interacting with them, and their love and excitement came through clearly, flowing from their hearts, because they are literally little children out to steal your heart with their cuteness. Everyone loved them, and the Hybrid Children were so excited! They talked about how much they love to play and sing, and how much they appreciate their Teachers, and how much they loved learning—and all in an excited tone like a four-year-old who has just petted a puppy for the first time. They answered lots of questions in their small-child expressions and scrunched up their little faces for emphasis, which resulted in my face being scrunched up reflectively. I will give you some of the questions and their answers to give you more examples of not only their views and style, but also to show how they differ from humans.

"We...don't really see you the way that you see each other. We sense you more than we see you at this particular juncture, because we have been trained to read resonances, to know the frequencies of the individuals who we interact with. And that is not only for our benefit and education, but it is a safety factor, for our energy is stronger than yours, and we would not like for your biology to short-circuit or to have any other negative effects. Because that doesn't helllp! That doesn't bring us closer to you! And that doesn't raise the

vibration of humanity up so we can freely interaaact. We want to come face-to-face! And we can't do that because youuuuuu and your planet aren't ready."

Hybrid Children channeled by Ray Heitman 6/1/25
https://www.youtube.com/watch?v=2tOkl6UUrpg&t=17s

One questioner asked, "Is there anything we can do to help us get ready sooner so you can come visit sooner?"

They answered, "It's all vibration. So we...our first thought is...Yes! Play more. Play more, play more, play more, all the time! But there is the, um, other aspects, such as doing your shadow work to find out what is holding you back. There are things which you store in your bodies and your memories which keep you down. Which do not allow you to fully flower. And you get nipped in the bud almost literally like that, because you do not...you have fears or doubts or things of that nature. And when those happen, you slide away from us. You don't come closer. So yes, if you do your work, and you, you ensure that you get to vibrate higher, then that makes it easier not only for us to connect, but for your energy to interact with others on your planet and bump them up too! Even if they don't know. So that will help everybody by you being at your besssst, and youuuuu being your vibrationalllll top tip-top shape."

Hybrid Children channeled by Ray Heitman 6/1/25
https://www.youtube.com/watch?v=2tOkl6UUrpg&t=17s

Another attendee asked, "I was just wondering if you do art on the ships?"

Their answer: *"Ooooooh! We, we play with lots of stuff! Yeah, we make...but not...not like you. (Deep breaths). We create lots of things, but they're not really physical things a lot. It, it is more energetic things like thought bubbles or ummmmm...or lots of games, lots of mental games. And we can share them, and pick who we choose to share them with, and not. It is part of learning our discernment and controlling, so we don't just broadcast to everybody. But um, we do like to create. We like to play, and then we like to animate those creations and make stories up around them. And give them their own reality that we can play with as mini gods, so to speak. Because the other children can see and experience what we are discussing and interacting with. And they can add their own, and often do, because it is a synchronous group. When we get an idea to make something, you'll find that lots of other ideas, lots of mental hands are coming in to help us build things. And then we give them life and see what they have to teach us."*

Hybrid Children channeled by Ray Heitman 6/1/25
https://www.youtube.com/watch?v=2tOkl6UUrpg&t=17s

They also shared a couple of their thoughts for the event attendees…

"We want people to learn more about us. The more people learn about us, the more people will learn to love us. And hopefully, they will play more so we can play with them sooner."

Hybrid Children channeled by Ray Heitman 6/1/25
https://www.youtube.com/watch?v=2tOkl6UUrpg&t=17s

"We have to do our studies. We have to make sure that we are prepared for meeting humans in your future. In our future, too, in ways. But we are more focused on the current now. We seldom try to

look farther than that because we do not have to. Our joy is in the moment, and the moment is in the Now."

Hybrid Children channeled by Ray Heitman 6/1/25
  https://www.youtube.com/watch?v=2tOkl6UUrpg&t=17s

Everyone at the event fell in love with them right then and there. Their energy was so pure and loving that even coming through a graying, bearded man, it delighted them all. And the Hybrid Children were just getting started filling those hearts with love. They kept coming through me several times a week, telling me more about the things which excited them and what they were doing in those darling voices like elementary-school children excited to tell about their day. And they are so lovingly consistent in their focus and demeanor, I was so enamored with them that I couldn't resist. And the unconditional love they exude will be shared with and for all beings on our planet. Their views and perspectives helped open my eyes and taught me much about our world. They are very intent on getting humanity to raise its vibrational frequency range enough to they can come and interact in person and then make Earth their home.

"The Hybrid Children are another species, although they are family. They are learning how to integrate themselves into the human framework so that you can have interspecies communications and relationships with other hybrid beings. That is part of the process of coming into awareness of your galactic family. The Hybrid Children have been specifically trained and are being educated to try to make the integration process of Earth into the broader galactic family more seamless. If we appeared to you tomorrow in our physical form, you may not like what you see, and it might be more challenging for you to accept that there are species like us out there somewhere. However, the Hybrid Children are almost indistinguishable physically from human children, or what we would call the sixth hybrid race children. And therefore, the integration of them into your society, your culture,

indeed your field of belief is going to be much more palatable. Initially, it will be the children who are being born now that will embark on those friendships or relationships with the Hybrid Children. They are a generation somewhat different in that way that they have that opportunity, but that does not mean to say that you will not meet the Hybrid Children yourself. Remember, you are the original stewards of the hybrid program who came in to specifically be conscious of all of this unfolding at this time. There is a mystery being unraveled here, and you have put yourself in the driver's seat for a reason."

Zariyah channeled by Aisling O'Donnell 3/21/24

https://www.youtube.com/watch?v=ZxcEuM9_-7A&t=3408s

To explain vibrational frequency range, it is representative of the amount of divine love energy which our bodily forms can handle. The amount of love we can hold. The higher the vibrational frequency we can hold in our hearts and bodily cells, the more love is able to flow through, and conversely, the lower the vibrational frequency range, the less a human is able to feel and show love. An example would be the higher your vibrational frequency, the brighter your auric field. Let's assume an angel's auric field would be a bright white, full as can be, with no other colors to dull its shine, and a being that is unable to receive or give love would be completely black and unable to emanate any light or love. The bright white light would be the "highest" any human could attain, but each negative thought or energy held within us will appear as a dark line upon our aura. Every instance of unresolved energy from traumas, arguments, hate, jealousies, mistreatments, fears, or injustices would darken our aura and limit our vibrational frequency, even if we are not consciously aware of them.

We all have varying degrees of darkness with our auric fields, or otherwise we would be angels! Our so-called "shadow" energy casts a shadow upon our aura, but every time we address and release those energies and beliefs which no longer serve us, we literally shine brighter and can receive and extend more love to others because we vibrate higher. Another example: Low-vibrational energies are analogous to a guitar string not tuned properly while we attempt to play a chord. No matter our skill level or intent, if we are not tuned to the clear resonance of the right vibration, we will sound off. Low-vibrational energies keep us from vibrating at our best love resonance, but once resolved, we come through loud and clear. The more we hold those shadow energies within us, the more out of tune or alignment we are with our divine resonance. But there are effective ways to release them, which I will address in a later chapter.

The "range" part of vibrational frequency range means the highest and lowest points of that frequency in wave form, which is a reflection of the ups and downs of the emotional states we experience. The Hybrid Children and extraterrestrials want us to play and sing and have fun all the time, or at least as often as possible, because it raises our core vibration and moves us closer to Open Contact. When our collective vibration gets high enough, they can come and play and love us face-to-face—what a party that will be! That vibrational level and celebration are a top priority for the Hybrid Children because they cannot start their planetary missions to help us fix our planet, improve our lives, and evolve into the best race we can be until they are allowed to come and play. Until then, they are diligent about learning as much as they can about us and our world each day, and interacting with as many of us as possible to anchor more of their love energy into our Earthly environment. Each interaction with Hybrid Children raises our vibration like adding hot coffee to a cold half a cup raises its temperature. They are learning all they can to help prepare for their missions once they come to Earth. Hopefully in 2028, but maybe not until 2030. It depends on us and our collective vibration. I will cover the timing of their arrival later.

"The most exciting hybrid program on Earth is the Hybrid Children program. There are Hybrid Children who are being trained in how to seamlessly integrate themselves into your Earth culture, into your Earth's atmosphere, into the level of density required to be on Earth at this time. That process is incremental. It is something that the Hybrid Children are acclimatizing to. What is exciting about that is that as you raise your vibrational frequency range with Gaia and the collective vibrational frequency range of the Earth rises, the hybrids have to do less work in terms of densifying to meet you where you are. In that sense, really, it is a co-creation. You are coming up, so to speak, and they are densifying to meet you, and that is where you will find that vibrational frequency bandwidth where you can be in physical together. It is somewhere between the fourth and fifth density."

Zariyah channeled by Aisling O'Donnell 12/23/23
www.youtube.com/watch?v=jMR6iB8GKCw&t=25s

In mid-October of 2025 I was told by the Future Pleiadians and Hybrid Children, and other beings in the dream state, I would be writing a book on the Hybrid Children as part of the Open Contact scenario and they would help me. I was so excited! I have been writing for quite some time and a collaboration with such loving beings was beyond my wildest dreams. It added another "dimension" to my relationship with both of those groups I channel and reaffirmed to me how important it was get this information out because of the frequency and resonance it will carry. My first efforts read like a reference manual, which it ended up being, as I realized I had written and informational book of the mind, and that would never be representative of the love of the Hybrid Children, so I had to try again and this time let it flow from the heart and help people understand Open Contact and beyond it as the acts of love they are. And love is energy behind this book and its writing has been a joyful and emotional cooperation.

The blessings I have received for not only being chosen for my relationship and roles related to Open Contact, but my appreciation at having this special relationship with the Hybrid Children, the darling ambassadors to our future, is something I feel I could never accurately portray in written form. At least the Hybrid Children only wanted "royalties of the heart" since they joked at one point early while editing the manuscript as I was going through their quotes stating humorously, "We wrote more of the book than you did!". That is a prime example of the love and playfulness they provide me through my connection with them, which continues to grow. I expect it to grow even more as my biology continues to be prepared to accommodate the beings I will encounter in my own personal extraterrestrial contact events and beyond. The same thing happening to you if you desire to be part of the Open Contact scenario or currently exploring or expanding your metaphysical gifts or purpose. And if not you, then more likely your descendants. It is all energy and our bodies must be prepared to handle it up to and including face to face, which is more love energy than we can currently handle as a species, and the Hybrid Children shall lead us.

And just who and what are these Hybrid Children who desire to bring abundant love to our planet? That is not a question with a simple answer. They are an example of the best humans can hope to become—humans without fears or misgivings about others, who do not harbor traumas or experiences that harmed them or haunt them. Humans without instilled societal or generational beliefs to keep us all from loving each other openly, unconditionally, and automatically, without thinking. Humans who innately desire to share, uplift, support, and love all beings—and not just humans, but all beings without exception. The Hybrid Children believe everything is made of divine love energy and therefore deserves to be loved, honored, respected, and given a chance to lead its best life. A very worthy ideal indeed, and one which will blossom on our planet in the future. I hope we can all see the value in that scenario.

In more practical terms, the Hybrid Children are a blend of human and extraterrestrial DNA, lovingly created to serve as a bridge between extraterrestrial races and humans, and vice versa. They are engineered to help humans evolve into a more unified, loving, heart-centered, higher-vibrational race. They are the intermediary and key to the next evolution of humanity into Homo galacticus—a spacefaring race alongside extraterrestrial species. A very big task! I know that is a lot to take in, and I understand why, but rest assured, they will help us get there with the help of many other loving spacefaring races. When their higher vibrational energy meets ours, it lifts us and delights us, and that impact is felt by us as deep, tangible love. They will literally bring out the love in us and build it into us as well, as they have done for me and those who have had the pleasure of connecting with them. I can tell you from personal experience, you will want more and more of that feeling. And their love energy does not fade over time. It is a love we will never tire of, and it nurtures our bodies, minds, and Souls. A quote from them on their creation:

"Everybody's different, and we're all even made from different parts, although lots of humans aren't really aware of all the parts that they come from. But that's okay too, because once after Open Contact, they can find out all they want."

Hybrid Children channeled by Ray Heitman 6/12/25

https://youtu.be/7U0Rfuk9vLU

And how do we do that? How do we get to experience them in person? The simple answer is by being the most authentic, loving beings we can be. To emulate the Hybrid Children in our everyday lives. Are you ready to receive more love? Are you ready to be more love? That is what it will take to bring them in, and the more we open ourselves to more love and broadcast more love, the sooner they will arrive.

"And we look forward to sharing that with you. It is a grand, grand, loving gesture. A huge step in consciousness to transcend an, an entire world into a higher vibrational realm. And thank you for being part of it. And thank you for listening to this message. And thank you for thanking us! (laughs) And we will, we are glad to bring you this information."

Hybrid Children channeled by Ray Heitman 6/24/25
https://youtu.be/vBKsxeu5mFY

Chapter One

Ray's Channeling Journey and Open Contact Involvement

My journey into nonphysical began before I could talk. My first memory was a five-minute déjà vu experience, which upset me greatly. The moment the déjà vu began, I became agitated because I knew my baby brother was going to have his tiny hand smashed flat under my dad's black shoe heel. My brother, who was born fifteen months after me, could not walk yet, so I was under two years of age. My mom was sitting on the couch, watching the *Mike Douglas Show*, while my brother slept on a blanket on the floor in front of her. I grew agitated when I recognized the beginnings of a series of events that I innately knew would lead to a large amount of pain for my brother. As these events progressed toward the feared outcome, I became increasingly upset, thinking the "big people" would see what was going to happen and stop it, but my mom kept doing what would lead to my brother's injury. She bounced me and held me, which upset me more because those were the exact things that would further the event I wished to avoid. When the phone rang, I silently begged her not to answer it, fearing it would lead to the dreaded event, but she answered regardless.

I knew my dad would be coming home soon and would make his way up the stairs into our kitchen. I recognized the phone conversation my mom was having as part of the sequence of events I was trying to get them to avoid. I caused enough of a fuss that my mom told the person on the phone she didn't know why I was so upset. My faith in big people was shaken because they didn't change their behavior to prevent anything from happening to my brother. They acted like they wanted to see my brother get hurt! My mom continued her phone call, and then I heard my dad's car pull up and his car door shut, just like in my vision. I started screaming in distress as loudly as I could. It was very traumatic. My mom told whoever she was talking to that she had to go and pick me up, asking me what was wrong, just like I had seen in my mind. My dad's measured steps resounded as he made his way up the steep stairs, and I screamed my little heart out! It was happening regardless of my outbursts. The big people did not understand. Reaching the top stair, my dad opened the door and asked what was wrong with Ray. My mom said she didn't know and handed me to him, and he asked me the same question as he lifted me high above his head and took a step back. As he did so, his heel came down on my brother's hand as he had awakened and crawled out into the kitchen and was right behind him. I saw his hand get squished flat in my mind and felt that pain. I was so confused, hurt, and angry. Why didn't the big people stop it from happening? Both my brother and I were crying relentlessly in a squall of emotion.

Somehow, I felt in that moment that the big people either did not know about those visions or didn't want me to know they knew. It changed me and how I viewed the world. I still knew about things, but I kept them more to myself, as those I did share were written off as "imagination" or "something I saw or heard somewhere." The fact is, my mom was terrified of esoteric and spiritual activity, but I trusted my experiences and was not dissuaded from having them, only from relaying them to others. Frequently, until I was about five years old, I had a vision of an invisible inverted pyramid shape balancing on my little index finger, with its base extending beyond the ceiling and roof. It seemed to hold all of creation and was an immense weight, but I just knew it was full of really big, heavy things, so I imagined planes, elephants, buses, firetrucks, and anything else I could think of filling it up. It did not dent my finger, which I found fascinating, and it moved with me when I moved my hand from side to side or up and down. I tried explaining it a couple of times to no avail, so eventually I stopped trying. But I kept enjoying my little secret.

Such precognitions crept in from time to time. I had two dogs tell me they were going to die while I was petting them, which really saddened me. And one died a couple of hours later when it got out and was run over by a motorcycle. The other one died the next day. One afternoon, I saw smoke and knew it was a car fire along a highway we were going to pass in another twenty or so miles, on a different highway than we were on, which caused my mom to yell at me. Not for saying it, but because she had seen enough and heard enough of my experiences and "tellings" to know those statements had value, and she was afraid of them. And of course, we saw a car on fire off the side of the highway on the way home. At least I got to say I told you so.

Those "weird" knowings kept happening, and then one summer day, when I was about thirteen, my mom and dad were both at work; neither my brother, who was reading a Hardy Boys book, nor my younger sister, who was playing with her horses, wanted to play with me. So I strolled out onto the side porch to see if there was anything interesting out there. The new home construction in our subdivision was paused, so there was nothing new to explore there, and then I saw a flock of common grackles towards the end of our backyard. I wondered why they moved their heads side to side while searching for food. Then I wondered just how accurate their beaks were, and no sooner had that thought entered my head than my consciousness flew into the matriarch of the flock!

I was stunned and knew my body was still on the porch leaning on the railing and watching, but my consciousness was inside the head of a bird! It was fantastic! I instantly knew where every other bird was and what they found to eat and what they would not eat (a green shiny beetle). I knew the spacing between each bird, and I knew the accuracy of their beaks was within a thousandth of an inch! I also sensed why they turned their head when foraging—it was so they always had an eye looking out for predators! Amazing. I enjoyed that experience in awe for a couple of minutes and wondered how long it would last. Then I wondered whether I could talk to them, which posed a bit of a dilemma, as I was sure they did not speak English. I wondered what word I could send to them telepathically to interact with them, which they would know, even if it was in English. Then my big, presumptuous mind happened upon the word "fly." I innately thought we both would know the meaning of that word, and I smiled inwardly, mentally picturing them flying and screaming FLY telepathically. Instantly, my consciousness flew back into my head as the flock immediately soared off in unison. I had cut short my wonderful experience with my impudence and gall, and desire to interact with them. I cursed myself a bit, but that experience and the wonder of it stayed with me. Of all the words or symbols I could have picked, I picked the one that would cause them to leave! I was beside myself and duly chastised myself for a minute, but the wonder and amazement of the experience took over, and I was beside myself with glee, replaying the event over and over in my mind. It was fantastic, and I had never heard of anyone else experiencing that kind of encounter.

Then, at age sixteen, my metaphysical journey began with a conscious adventure after a commanding voice of nonphysical origin saved my life and opened the door to explorations beyond the physical plane. I grew up in a cricket-quiet small town of several hundred people in mostly old houses, which was too small for a stoplight. Our house was in one of those newer subdivisions that had sprung up amidst a vast grove of young maple trees that had encroached and eventually filled in the former crop fields farmed by previous generations, where the subdivision was now situated about thirty miles south of St. Louis, Missouri. In the early 1970s, the new Highway 55 had been open for a number of years, but like the town, there wasn't much to see, especially at night, because there were no streetlights. It was a warm summer's night with a chorus of a million insects resounding in my ears. I was returning alone from one of my frequent trips to my four cousins' home, about five miles away from my house, in the newer subdivision. That magical house was where my brother and I spent many of our evenings playing cards, darts, and generally hanging out and having a lot of fun pertinent to the throes of energetic youth.

I learned early that if I gave my parents things to brag about, my life worked out pretty well, and being a straight-A student and a top-notch youth bowler while managing my part-time job at the bowling alley, coupled with always getting my home chores done, enabled me to enjoy "no curfew" in high school. An hour or so after midnight that Friday in July, I was on my way home, windows down, radio off, and listening to the familiar creaks and rattles of the tired engine from my 1972 Datsun B210 station wagon settle in after I stretched each gear to its utmost limit. I experienced the freedom and power of all the speed it could muster. The stars were out, and there were no lights along the route to obscure their twinkle in those days except the entrance to the bowling alley and a distant billboard many miles away. It was too hot to have the windows up with no air conditioning, and too noisy to hear the radio with the windows down at highway speeds. I can still see the darkness of the road and then the darkness beyond my headlights, hidden in shadow at the edge of the grassy median.

It was my first car, and it was nice to feel the freedom, as I was thrilled to make it go as fast as it could, as often as I could. There was no moon to cast a glint on the windshield this night, and I could just make out the details of the Main Street bridge over the highway in my high beams as I neared my exit. I was ready to signal to get off the highway, but thought how silly it was to do so since there was no one to see my signal anyway. It was at that instant that I had a profound experience which undoubtedly changed and prolonged my life.

A powerful voice suddenly yelled full force at me inside my skull: "PULL OVER!!! It filled my car, and I didn't just hear it—I felt it. The urgency, the immediacy, and a split second later, the message was repeated more strongly. "PULL OVER!!!" So loud, I jumped in my seat. So forceful and immensely authoritative, I was immediately jolted into action, and in the face of common sense and no visible danger or reason, I obeyed, skidding hard on the cinder gravel and skidding to a stop a dozen or so feet from the exit, which would lead me to my home less than a mile away. The immediacy and power of the requests startled and scared me. I had so many questions and wanted to know why I was yelled at, by whom, or what. I quickly tried to make sense of my surreal experience, but its purpose was soon known as a large black four-door sedan sped down the exit ramp towards me, going the wrong way with no headlights on. I'm guessing they saw my car on the shoulder, or maybe came to their senses, for they braked hard and left skid marks just off the highway, making a U-turn and pulling off in the right direction with their loud voices trailing, leaving me alone and startled on the side of the road.

I was shaking. I had so many thoughts and emotions, all yelling at once, trying to crowd out the others. I was sobbing heavily. Crying at my good fortune. Crying because I could have died! Crying in anger that those assholes could've killed me! I was so, so unbelievably grateful for the message I had received. I cried for a long time, taking off my T-shirt and using it as a tissue out of necessity. Then gratitude won out. I was celebrating a miracle so beyond what was "supposed" to be possible, I didn't think people would believe me. So many thoughts on so many levels. I had all of those things, but they settled at some point into the overwhelming curiosity of...*What was that?* With that thought, the calming realization that there was something outside of the world lovingly watching over me, and it was there for me in my time of greatest need.

With my Catholic upbringing, angels were the first thought that came to mind, but I didn't want to guess. I wanted to know the source and how it had managed to manifest that profound communication with me, whether I could keep it with me all the time, and all the other things I didn't know were possible. Thoughts of knowing this process had occurred before, many times, paraded at light speed through my head. The realization that whoever or whatever saved me had been trying to get me to listen my entire life. I had protectors, and my life had purpose, or it would not have been saved. I wept with joy at the revelation and received what I can only consider to be an overflowing of divine love, gushing forth, divine tears flowing once more. I have no idea how long I sat there in a warm spiritual glow, sobbing on the side of the highway in the middle of the night. I was beholden in that special moment until the deep sighs of excitement, exhilaration, exhaustion, and release finally came and subsided, and the sobs left me. I was more drained than I can ever remember feeling, and I experienced a clarity and spiritual acuity I had never felt before. I knew I had achieved a significant awakening. A door had not just been revealed, but flung aside, and my spiritual journey had begun.

I had awareness and undeniable personal proof of the existence of, and connection to, an entity beyond the physical world who loved and protected me. And shows up in my time of need. A great ball of realization, confirmation, and expression of gratitude was inside that amazing gift of love, all culminating from an incredible experience that altered my life forever in positive ways. Something I couldn't explain saved my life in a way I couldn't understand. My ego basked in the knowledge: "I must be pretty important." And right then and there, I was determined to find the answers to the questions my upbringing couldn't answer.

And I did find those answers, and they opened up even more doors of exploration I didn't consciously know existed. My journey took me to and through the Bible (twice) and religious texts from a handful of other religions, I also found wisdom in Wayne Dyer, Ram Dass, Jack Canfield, Abraham-Hicks, Deepak Chopra, Jane Roberts and Seth, Zig Ziglar, Gay & Katie Hendricks, Rumi, Thich Nhat Hanh, Neville Goddard, Richard Bach, and others great and small. Their gifts of knowledge revealed more of the world beyond the physical world in which we live our conscious day-to-day lives, and once I started that journey, I knew it would never end. I grew to love and enjoy the parts of myself I had never consciously known existed, and I was shown that acknowledging and loving them was a key to deepening my connection with them, which was really about remembering more about who I am in a much larger, grander context. A true "coming home" feeling I have been fortunate enough to follow for the rest of my life.

But it was the Seth material, channeled by Jane Roberts and her husband Robert Butts, that provided the most profound insights and laid the foundation for my life today. I found those books in 1987 as I scoured every book fair and garage sale for science fiction, which was the majority of my ever-present thirst for reading. And the Seth books came to me like a well-planned daisy chain: just as I finished one, another would become available somehow. An obvious signal of coordination and timing, which fell into Seth's teaching, "There are no coincidences." Everything was all part of a great plan, which is still unfolding, and gloriously so. And with my ego, I decided I could channel another entity as Jane Roberts did, and if not vocally per Seth, I knew it was possible to allow other beings to share in my physical experience, so I invited any beneficial being to come and share my experience. They came right away and never stopped coming to this very day, and at times they made their presence known by doing things beyond physics and my own abilities.

For instance, I am not a singer, and each baseball game I went to I patriotically croaked out the "Star Spangled Banner," and having season tickets in the bleacher seats at Busch Stadium, many fans around me had heard me give it my all, and I imagine several were happy when the song ended so they did not have to suffer through my singing attempts. But one day, as soon as the music to our national anthem started, a perfect baritone emerged from my throat, and I sang the whole anthem flawlessly and with passion! It was good enough to turn heads and mouths to fall open from several sections away. The singing and voice were incredible! I was stunned, overjoyed, and weeping. It wasn't me, but it came through me, and I had no idea who it may have been, but it was incredible. Several other season ticket holders around me said, "I didn't know you could sing!" I had to tell them, "I can't!" I sat and cried for several minutes at having that miracle bestowed upon me.

Another time, former billiards and pool legend Minnesota Fats decided to pay me a visit. Many nights after bowling, a small group of us went to a buddy's house to play pool in his basement. I am an average pool player at best, and usually miss almost as many shots as I make. I felt Minnesota Fats come in, and he identified himself right away. He wanted to play pool again, and he had been dead for several years by that time. When my turn came, I cleared the rest of the balls on the table and sank the eight ball to win the game. As "luck" would have it, it was my turn to break. I hit a ball in, then proceeded to quickly dispatch all of the other balls for my team, with only the eight ball remaining. I had never "run the table" in my entire life, meaning gotten all of "my" balls in without the competition even getting a chance to shoot. My friends were amazed at my sudden prowess and skill, not only at how quickly, confidently, and cleanly I made each shot, but also at how I positioned the cue ball after each one to make the next shot easier.

As I looked the pool table over, I noticed there was no clean shot to hit the eight ball, as the opponent's seven balls were on the table and in the way of a direct shot. I immediately saw the solution and called a double bank and the eight ball in the side pocket next to me without even checking the angles involved. My opponents and spectators laughed, saying things like they couldn't even see that shot and that my luck had run out. One looked closely at the path to the side pocket I had indicated and said he couldn't see how the eight ball would fit between two other balls in the way. I laughed, knowing my "secret weapon" was in charge and casually shot the cue. It went between several balls, hit the first bank, proceeded to the second, and then gently clipped the eight ball, sending it to the side pocket. It had only about 1/8-inch clearance on each side to fit between two balls near the side pocket. It negotiated them cleanly and slowed slightly before dropping dramatically into the side pocket. I was stunned and elated in equal parts. Minnesota Fats thanked me for letting him come in and left, and I burst into tears at being so fortunate at that gift having been bestowed upon me, even if no one else would believe it. I was congratulated profusely on my amazing feat, and I told everyone, "It was like Minnesota Fats took over my body." I have experienced many such magical moments with connections from "beyond," some I know and many I don't. Two of the notables I know who visited were Harry Chapin and Mark Twain.

The exploration of Seth and the advent of the internet led me to Seth groups online, and I joined a monthly in-person Seth group in 2017, which I still attend to this day. It was in one of those groups that I was led to befriend an excellent channeler in 2019, Kathleen Whitehead. We grew closer, and then she told me she thought I would be a good fit for their small channeling group. I had no idea how it would affect my life and point my journey of exploration in new directions, but I soon found out.

I joined that group, which was focused around a group of entities called Aspects of Love, and had the impetus to transcribe the channeling sessions, which I did for the next two years. Each week was an amazing experience, and I learned a great deal and became acquainted with the vastness and differentiation of the extraterrestrial races, both physical and nonphysical. I was in awe each week, and rewatching each session, spending time absorbing those experiences through authenticating the transcripts really helped that vibrational energy seep in. After two years, I sensed my time in that group was done, and the very next week, another excellent channeler offered free sessions on the same day and time as the group I had just left. I joined Aisling O'Donnell and the entity she channeled, Zariyah, a nonphysical being from the Orion constellation. Those sessions had even greater depth and information than any I had ever experienced, and I quickly began transcribing as many of them as I could for two years as well. I learned so much about how our planet and the various races came to be, and about their roles in humanity's future, which only whetted my desire to learn more and more. During this time, I also started following other channelers and expanded the number of Seth groups I followed on social media. I was being bestowed with high-vibrational content relevant to enhancing my spiritual journey and providing a more solid foundation for what was to come.

In 2024, Aisling took a hiatus from channeling, and one of the members of our small group said he had recently begun channeling and he could take over, but only every other week. I took it upon myself to find other friends who channeled, and they all flowed like magic and became part of our group, and High Vibe Channeling was born 9/17/24. It was, and still is, directed by higher realms. In early October of 2024, during a High Vibe Channeling session, I told a channeled entity I was interested in starting my own channeling journey and was told, "You already have a Tall White, which is a being from Alpha Centauri who has been on Earth since before Earth was formed, um, who wanted to speak through you." I was very excited. When another channeler friend of mine told me the Yahyel named Raven had told him three times to contact me because she wanted to speak with me to give me a channeling lesson, I immediately worked out the logistics. I was quite excited not only at having other entities wanting to connect with me, but also at getting a channeling lesson from one was just fantastic. I was even more excited by the time that day came. The lesson took about seven minutes on 10/16/24, and I began my own personal channeling journey the very next morning.

The lesson itself was very straightforward. It involved establishing a routine of having a set time each day in a place where I could sit, relax, and be free of distractions with a pen and paper, and then clear my mind, state that my intention was to connect, and "I am open." Then write down every thought that came into my mind for twenty or thirty minutes or as long as the connection lasted. The dedication and desire are important communications to any entity considering coming through, in my opinion. Another channeled entity in a High Vibe Channeling session told me a spot in nature would aid my connection, so I picked a spot on a log that had fallen over the creek behind my home. It became my meditation spot, beautifully selected as the sun shone through the trees, with birds singing and the energy of the creek and foliage nurturing me; the solitude of my perch was a captivating gift in itself. I did as I was told, and a consciousness came through telepathically almost immediately after I said, "I am open," by replying, "We hear you." The voice urged me to be patient, as this was a process, not a light switch, and to "feel for us." It seemed to speak just as fast as I was able to write in a loving, direct tone. After a few sentences, it asked me to stop writing and just relax and breathe deeply. I did as I was told and let the sun bathe upon my upturned face as energies cruised through my body as it was being made ready to receive their energy. They told me they had to "adjust" me, and they had to get comfortable with me, too. They talked about my chosen spot and that the writing "remembers for you." I felt pressure behind my eyes, but I was too happy to care about any discomfort. They said the deep breathing activates "things" to make it easier for them. They asked me to breathe them into my heart, as that is where the communication begins.

Those beings who came through the next morning were not the Tall Whites I expected, but another group that said they were beings of love and light, so I dubbed them Beings of Light. They are non-physical entities who specialize in bending and blending light into other structures. The lessons progressed beyond automatic writing with a pen and paper, but those early sessions held value, so I chronicled them in my YouTube channel, Channeling Beings of Light. On 11/21/24, I progressed to vocalized channeling of the Beings of Light and joyously never looked back. The messages they provided were profound, and from a loving perspective I found hard to resist, which awed me. Like me, others felt like the messages were personally for them. I believe this is because their love and messages resonate with something innate within us, as they are focused on helping us realize we are so much more than we know. Always guiding us with a loving hand to remember more of our true nature and grander selves as beings created from love.

My channeling connections have grown considerably since then. In February of 2024, in another channeling session, I learned how to connect to the Pleiadians. I later learned that I had a female counterpart in that group, and they were a nonphysical seventh-density group in a timeline approximately four hundred years in our linear "future," so I labeled them Future Pleiadians. The initial connections were a bit rough on my body as their energy was so strong. It had me thrashing around like I was hooked to a live high-voltage wire upon connection and for a couple of minutes after they left as well. They told me to connect with them only once per week at first so my body could recover, and they worked on my biology in each session to help me handle their energy more easily. I do not know what those adjustments were, but I assumed they knew what they were doing and openly approved and accepted whatever they chose to provide. I have since learned that almost every extraterrestrial or nonphysical being or group has a specific energy which our bodies must be able to accept, and the energy residuals after that connection recedes may take a bit of time to subside. It was not comfortable to do so, but I did what I was told, and it gradually got easier. After three weeks, I was able to shorten the time frame between connection attempts, and in a couple of months, they were smooth, and I could bring them in vocally in mere seconds. Channeling Future Pleiadians was my second YouTube channel after Channeling Beings of Light. The Future Pleiadians group was so loving and always urging us to be more loving and to do things that were focused on raising our vibration and expanding our identity and sense of self, usually in a playful way.

They proved to be instrumental in my channeling expansion, as they were focused on obtaining as many perspectives on Open Contact as they could, and I thought they meant human perspectives, but I was to learn that was a huge understatement. They were able to take my consciousness to another planet (Ess-Kadaya) and deliver profound and moving meditations for our High Vibe Channeling group, with whom they are a favorite. They also opened up and maintain a communication conduit that other beings could use to experience not only humanity through me, but physicality and my Earthly environment as well. And their love for me enabled the Hybrid Children to connect with me. That was a gift larger than anything I could imagine, and they helped me understand the role I was playing and would play in the future, and in Open Contact.

In early May of 2025, I participated in a CE-5 meditation (Close Encounters of the 5th kind) via Zoom, conducted by two friends who were visiting Mount Shasta, California. During that meditation, I was contacted by a Tall White and telepathically given the "call sign" to dial them in: placing the back of my hand on my left knee and opening and closing my hand three times. As the meditation continued, the Tall White answered every question and request given by the person leading the meditation and continuously worked on my biology, so I would be able to handle their vibration. At the end of the meditation, I received a "download," and he packaged my experiences together so he could share them with others. He gave his name as "Being" and told me he was chosen for this role and did not volunteer, but a "decision-maker" chose him, whatever that means. Here are some of my notes after the experience.

I felt a presence on the underside of my arms and upper back; it felt like my spine was being stretched. He later told me he was beside me and didn't need telepathy to learn about me. I get the impression the Tall Whites disdain language as unnecessary and cumbersome. They can take in great swaths of information at a glance, and they think in more grandiose terms in a seemingly impartial manner, ignoring the various types of entities and concentrating more on maintaining the flow of divine energy. They are not used to sharing info for the sake of sharing, entertainment, or the education of others except as necessary. They are "support," but this one, among others, is willing to talk now. They are very matter-of-fact, and their perspectives are enlightening. They anticipate and fill in "gaps" because it is what their race does. They desire to learn more about humans before humans achieve a high enough vibrational frequency range to be able to detect other energies around them, like the ones the Tall Whites emit, so they can relate to them more effectively once that ability to detect them is commonplace amongst humans.

They were proactive in raising awareness among humanity before humanity discovered them on its own, and were required to learn about us to formulate and revise those plans. It was part of what changes we humans can expect after the so-called shift of ascension. To the Tall Whites, everything is about efficiency and necessity, and they desire every energy and expression of it to flow perfectly, so they focus on foreseeing and remedying incongruities and barriers to energy flows for the benefit of all consciousness interacting with those energies. There is no question about anything they do, and they are not fond of physical comparisons, especially to humans. Their perspective and focus are intense. They do more than just provide support, but in a sense, they are maintenance and advisors for a variety of energies and a multitude of beings as well.

Some messages from them: *"We trade perspectives with each other as you would switch TV channels, only seamlessly. We have a fondness for manifesting physically to interact with those energies which are analogous to us, like nature, Gaia. We are free there and unencumbered from expectations or duties, as our work is energetically behind the veil. The trivialities of humanity are below our level of understanding, but we accept all as valid. We are not curious as we have all relevant info we need. There is art in our flow and practices, and it is part of our 'being' makeup, but for our own ends and appreciations, and may be experienced by those who are able to perceive and appreciate it."* They continued, *"We imagine the pieces which 'fit' in realities. Like making a recipe better. Engineering a smoother ride. Removing impingements to ensure a fuller range of motion. We flow through what flows through us. The choice of sharing is novel to us in ways. As we are like water and go where reality takes us, and find our level of being. We do not seek to understand why anyone would withhold anything needed by another. We do not need to understand those things which are not 'us.' We merely need to know of them to take them into account as necessary. Like having extra chair available in case unexpected guests arrive. Since humans will become aware they share 'their' planet with us and others, we have begun a more noticeable exploration of humankind. A marketing plan of sorts, if you will. We need to ease people into us, and we need to learn not to ignore those superfluous things which are important to humans. The consideration of "relevance to others" is out of sync with our natural rhythms, but we change as necessary, of course. Because we have been silent, do not underestimate our intelligence."*

Tall Whites channeled by Ray Heitman May 2025

There is much more to tell about the Tall Whites, and this is just an overview. They will become more active and prominent in our future, and have learned quite a bit by analyzing and following me and members of our High Vibe Channeling group, who all volunteered to be part of their education. They have also begun dictating a book through me, have given me instruction on how it is to be structured, editing parameters, and have shown it to me in completed form in print is too small for me to see anything clearly. I look forward to seeing the finished version and working with the Tall Whites in the future.

And during May 2025, the Hybrid Children requested I channel them, and the Future Pleiadians readily agreed to facilitate that connection. Here is a quote from the Future Pleiadians about that request.

"We are happy to have this opportunity to relay our messages to whomever encounter them, and may they resonate deeply and uplift you in some ways. Now the channel has asked us to help him connect with the Hybrid Children, who just today have requested that he channel them as they would like to have a deeper relationship and a more active relationship with the channel. They are a delightful group of children, and several have come forth to interact with the channel when he prepares for his sessions. It is a great joy to see such natural expressions of joy and love, and to have them so pure without the tainted low vibration which are predominant in many humans and Earth cultures. While today is not the day to bring in the Hybrid Children, we will facilitate this connection. We will add our input and expertise in bringing them forth. It will be a joyous occasion, as interactions with the Hybrid Children are very energetic. And with them so excited and loving to have this connection, and with the channel so excited and loving and excited about this connection, and looking forward to it, it will be a joy to merge these loving entities so that they may explore more of each other in a more direct fashion."

Future Pleiadians channeled by Ray Heitman 5/11/25
https://www.youtube.com/watch?v=Y-F0mRCmNjI

After the Hybrid Children, things kept expanding, and as I later learned, I was being readied to handle even stronger vibrational energy and more diverse energies, too. It was and is part of the plan, or my mission, so to speak. In August of 2025, the Tall Whites told me to perform a fire ceremony and that they would guide me through every step of the process. Since the Tall Whites only do what is absolutely necessary, with the emphasis on "absolutely," I agreed. They instructed me that they would come through via channeling the next day, and for me to record that session, and they would explain more about the ceremony and the preparation, which they did.

I was told to take a specific bag I had, and was shown a mental picture of it, and then get three red leaves, four specific nuts, and about eighteen pieces of wood from four different trees or so. I asked each of those items if they would like to be part of the ceremony, and they all agreed and volunteered, while others chose to stay where they were. There were not that many red leaves in the forest, but I was led to them, just as I was guided to all of the items selected to be part of the ceremony. Each item I gathered gave me information about what benefit it was going to add to the ceremony. Some were for wisdom, some for the forest spirits, some for the beings to join the ceremony, some were to maintain the high vibration it would generate, some were to represent the land, sky, water, and fire. Each later told me exactly where and how to place them when I was preparing to put them in the fire pit for the ceremony. I gave reverence at all times. Lots of wisdom came in from the ones who called to me to join in the ceremony. I was to do a ceremonial smoke offering to the four directions, sky, and earth, and to face eastward.

This is what the Tall Whites told me about the ceremony:

"You have asked of the ceremony. It is energetic. The ceremony is in the symbols you create with the movements, the actions, the words, the thoughts, the intentions, the joinings from surrounding energies, and those added to combine to be recognized outside your reality. In a way to signal readiness and enable more such energies to be absorbed or received freely from Source in its manifestations. This is an opportunity for, and a proving ground for those who are interested but not persuaded in the potential actions which are to come before you. Your responses shall negate some options, reassure others. And although the outcomes are always determined in ways in which that is expressed to you, the glory is in each action which contributes to it. In your ways, a divine breath celebrated with each

blow into the balloon until it reaches the diameter or shape you desire. You are a divine breath being played out as you move throughout that which you would interpret as infinite limb, lungs of possibilities we will say. But in this realm of possibility, some fall under relevance, for they lead to avenues of expression which are not only desired, but desire to be experienced in ways which are unknown because they cannot be known by you in this level. But know no entity keeps anything from you. You and your kind are adored and are welcome to all of the gifts that are available to you. We desire to be more direct and give this, and give you more support, but you must allow, intend, and in some ways agree and support a connection beyond your typical physical reality. The ceremony will not occur in your physical reality. It is designed to allow greater introspection from further distances, we will say, and to allow certain energies to come to you in ways they choose. And that itself is part of the ceremony for all changes as you change, and those reactions can be extrapolated, interpreted, as patterns and variations are frequently known to help ascertain vastly different methods and avenues of exploration."

Tall Whites channeled by Ray Heitman, Summer of 2025

After the ceremony was complete, I was indeed a different person. Vast fields of information were open to me. I felt as if I just *knew* things and why they were the way they were, and more. It was as if blinders had been removed, or I had been given access to a tremendous nonphysical search engine. Many beings came and experienced with me in a nonphysical state during the ceremony and bodily after the ceremony was done. The Tall Whites told me the ceremony was to allow the Inner Earth beings to connect with me, which they did soon after. In the weeks that followed, two or more different entities explained that the ceremony had made me into a "portal" or access point for beings and energies to enter the physical realm and me with greater ease, in effect, making me analogous to a train station with lots of comings and goings of which I was mostly unaware. However, I chose this physical incarnation to be of service to all consciousness, and that is how my role is playing out, but in much grander fashion than I could have ever imagined. I was stunned and humbled at the many gifts I was given, and quite overwhelmed with love at times, also.

Afterwards, the Future Pleiadians remarked, *"We are finding this a refreshing view. It is a layered gathering. And a layer upon layer to get through, but the intent and desire help, and create as well."*

The Inner Earth beings came through the next week, and soon I was able to do what I termed open invitation channeling. Where the Future Pleiadians would open the floodgates, and any interested beings could come and interact in our group sessions. They could experience what it was like to be physical and human if they wished, as they had free access to my memories and senses. Their perspectives were mind-blowing and provided numerous insights into the diversity of other forms of consciousness and physical beings that are out there in our universe and beyond it. In total, more than one hundred different beings or groups have come through me in channeling, and that list keeps growing. Some do not provide names, as they are not important to them and not necessary for them to communicate. Outside our physical world, different beings and/or forms of consciousness are recognized by their energy signatures and vibrational frequencies, and names are not needed or desired. I look forward to my continued roles in Open Contact and in building awareness of not only the Hybrid Children, but the love coming to our planet and futures, and about the beings involved in those events. You can find many of these videos and all of the quotes from the Hybrid Children in this book on my YouTube channels: High Vibe Channeling, Channeling Hybrid Children, Channeling Future Pleiadians, and Channeling Beings of Light, and on the High Vibe Channeling and Channeling Hybrid Children Facebook pages also.

Summary

Thank you for being with me and us on this journey. Not just by adding your energy and focus to this book, which is really a cocreation of many beings and energies contributing their vibrations and guiding not only its creation but also the ongoing connection. My path will extend well past Open Contact. But you and I have chosen to incarnate in this time to be part of the changes humanity and our planet will experience, just like the Hybrid Children have. It is an exciting time, and there are millions and millions of beings assisting us and helping us to reach a vibrational frequency level where they can safely and more efficiently interact with us. Our story is just beginning, and many galactic races took millions and millions of years to achieve the unified consciousness we are on the brink of. Humans will accomplish that level of achievement in less than 500,000 years from when the first modern humans were created by an extraterrestrial race known as the Anunnaki, who mixed the DNA of existing primates with their own. No wonder we have so many extraterrestrials and energies focused on us! We are truly a miracle of creation and the best party in town. Since we are spirit energies having a human experience, part of the reality we have chosen to incarnate into means that we do not remember we are energy beings and part of an infinite consciousness, but the illusion of our reality is so involved and complex from our human perspective that we believe we are finite physical beings.

Most humans have yet to understand, in essence, that we have come from a place of deep forgetting, which was the path our souls chose to expand and learn in. As a race, transcending that idea and overcoming our tragedies and failings at achieving a unified planet to actually doing so, and growing into a race that will reach the stars and help other civilizations earn their space wings. In a couple of centuries or so, humans will take on the roles of some of the extraterrestrial races observing and helping us, and to aid other civilizations in reforming their societies to benefit and enhance all life on their planets. We will experience a greater diversity of beings off-world than we have ever had on Earth. And you chose to be here to experience it. So do your best to raise your vibration by emulating the Hybrid Children as much as possible as often as possible. It is the best we can do. I will leave you with one of my quotes, which I believe forms a fitting end to this story, which is just the beginning in many ways.

"As we begin to incorporate more of the Hybrid Children into our lives, our lives will become, and continue to become, more joyful from that point onward. You need only experience them to feel the truth in this. They are more than hope for the future; they are our way and our guides to our future."

Orion, channeled by Leslie Stewart 12/7/25. (Personal Session)

Chapter Two
Why Are They Coming?

Why are they coming? The easy answer is because they love us and want to help us, just like their extraterrestrial creators and Teachers have been nurturing them since before they took their first breath. That is their purpose of being, the reason they were created, and the reason they are coming to Earth. To share love and to help us grow in many ways to be happier, healthier, and more unified than ever in our existence. To help us handle the higher energies of the extraterrestrial races so we may freely accept their love and guidance. In short, they are coming to help us become more like the Hybrid Children. To comprehend the roles the Hybrid Children will play in our future, it helps to understand the larger scope of changes looming for humanity and our planet. That is a different love story, one which involves transforming our current societies into ones that openly participate and exhibit planetary unity and, most of all, deep love for all consciousness. That is not a pipe dream, but our coming future and the new world we are ushering in. If you ignore the media, you can feel the undercurrents of the wellspring of truth. The current power structures and leadership are fading and will fall, and those changes are already becoming more apparent on our planet. Maybe not in the ways most people expect, and certainly not the way it is portrayed in our media. But after we remove those propping up the things which are no longer working for all, we, and that dream shall receive the help and guidance of galactic partners, the extraterrestrials. But not until we have made hard choices and are moving in unison in the direction of love.

That will happen globally in 2027 through what is termed Open Contact, but let's look at this from our human perspective. Please keep an open mind that this information is not common knowledge currently. Extraterrestrials have been involved with our planet since before our planet was created, and they have been guiding and watching us from their loving perspectives just as we watch infants grow and learn to walk, communicate, and become self-sufficient. Those beings love us, and they know we have to be open to receiving their love and guidance before we will fully accept it and make it our own. And just as we let our toddlers fall and learn about their environment by exploring it step by precious step, humans have been exploring different social, economic, religious, and governmental structures for thousands of years. Think of all the different civilizations and forms of government and religion that have risen up, stood tall, and fallen. Baby steps. And we have tried again and again and again. Now is the time we learn to walk so the extraterrestrials can not only help us run but also fly. A new cycle has begun.

"The Hybrid Children are part of a gradual project of allowing humanity to step by step acclimatize to different frequencies, acclimatize to different types of consciousness, and recognize that there is a grand process of becoming and integrating into a galactic alliance. The Hybrid Children, because they will be directly related to you while still upgraded, you could say represent that initial step in integrating new types of energy. They will guide humans to become more intuitive, more honest, more authentic in their expression, more creative and even telepathic. They will have different ways of communicating that will startle humans and naturally tap into some psychic abilities through proximity. . . They will catalyze many processes of great healing and simultaneously help you to recognize how much untapped potential has always existed within you psychically."

The Pleiadian Council by Dante "Starshine" Filipini 3/12/26

https://www.youtube.com/watch?v=rE6-fZ5SRaI&t=5s

New organizations and societal focuses which honor, respect, and support all life upon our planet will be created and prioritized worldwide. For all life, even the smallest forms of it. A new beginning where the mind no longer leads, but is secondary to the heart and fulfills the heart's mission of loving intent. That is where previous attempts to govern and lead have failed. They lost the heart-based initiatives that served the many by instead focusing on individual freedoms, which were not aligned with those missives. That is where the extraterrestrials come in. That is where we need their expert assistance and loving hand. They will help gradually. Easing their way into our awareness as more and more information comes to light about them and their history with Earth and humans. The truth will come out eventually, and the pace of "disclosures" will not be under the control of those who wish to conceal and misrepresent their aims much longer. The number of spaceship sightings will increase significantly in 2026 and continue to rise. More sightings and information will come to light to help shift millions of people from denial of extraterrestrials' existence to "what if," and others from acceptance of their existence to excitement at having tangible proof of their existence.

It is all part of a mission being guided by those who desire to help humanity grow, and the Hybrid Children are an intermediary, a necessary bridge, to help build acceptance of them and their intent. To help show humans better ways of being, thriving, and taking care of our planet. They are the love we need to heal, and they are extremely well prepared for their roles. We will find them irresistible and bring them into our hearts, as they are the perfect beings to help us see what and how the extraterrestrial knowledge and technologies can do for us and all life forms on the planet. Once we experience and desire those wonders, and then ask for them, they will help humanity grow in new ways. And hope will return on a large scale across the globe, spawning a tidal wave of progress. And the Hybrid Children will be in the thick of it because they will enable humanity to love more and spread that love to all corners of the globe.

"We just wanted to add our loving embrace to all of you. And you, too, can have this experience. It is ready and waiting for you. You merely have to order it and wait for the table, well, you have set the table, and wait for the food to arrive! And we will meet you then."

Hybrid Children channeled by Ray Heitman 10/29/25
   https://youtu.be/QlMWBZDO9w8

"And we look forward to sharing that with you. It is a grand, grand, loving gesture. A huge step in consciousness to transcend an, an entire world into a higher vibrational realm. And thank you for being part of it. And thank you for listening to this message. And thank you for thanking us! (Laughs) And we will, we are glad to bring you this information."

Hybrid Children channeled by Ray Heitman 6/24/25
   https://youtu.be/vBKsxeu5mFY

Chapter Three

How Will They Help Us?

If you asked the Hybrid Children how they would help humanity once they arrive on our planet, they'd tell you by opening our hearts and getting us to play more. To be more like them. They will do that, but to help your understanding, I asked them specifically how they would help us, and this is what they said…

"We know you (Uncle Ray) asked us how we would help. And there are many ways which we will do that. But the main thing is by helping humans realize who and what they can be. To…um…show them more of what they can aspire to be, and to get that concept, that dream, and make it real. Because right now, humans do not believe that they can love unconditionally. They even have problems loving their children unconditionally, or their pets at sometimes. But that is something that is going to sink in. It will be a realization. It will become a knowing. It will become a practice. It will become a lifestyle."

Hybrid Children channeled by Ray Heitman 12/28/25

https://www.youtube.com/watch?v=pTNfiafbbsg

I am so looking forward to that! The benefits humanity will reap from the coming of the Hybrid Children are many-layered, even ethereal. Let's visualize being imbued with the ability to play God for a day, and being asked how you would help a fickle humanity transform our race and planet from the inside out. Being loving and compassionate, you would most likely express your desires to humanity in a broad spectrum of desired changes, and then provide humans the specifics of how to best accomplish those goals, and watch and hope those desires would be followed and accomplish the changes you hoped for, while giving a helping hand and guidance where needed. Your desire for a truly loving world where each being feels loved and has a chance to thrive, perhaps. But with free-willed humans, you would have to do it in a way that would be widely accepted by them in order to bring about lasting change. Otherwise, old paradigms and power factions may reassert themselves. That requires a well-defined integration plan, as a quick fix would not hold or be sustainable. You would have to show and prove to the masses that the coming changes would not only be possible but also work for all, and you would help them find faith and purpose.

That analogy will help you grasp the scope of the extraterrestrials' missions and the role the Hybrid Children play in introducing us and guiding us toward becoming the best race of beings we can be. To change humanity from the inside out, so we lead from the heart, not from mindful fears. To free our minds and societal structures from selfish aims and control mechanisms that can be manipulated for the benefit of the few to broader, more loving ideals that benefit everyone and everything. Things like free energy, new ways of healing and nourishing our bodies and the planet, and our spirits. This is what the Hybrid Children had to say about their roles as teachers and living on Earth:

"Schoolrooms of the future. To learn, and to play, and to teach! Yes. We will be, and we know that will be...that may be difficult for some who have...children who are teaching them, but we are well-equipped and have open hearts and understanding minds to help any who are interested and intent on learning to master to the best of their abilities whatever skills and services we have to offer. There are

physical limitations, of course, but the ideas will help birth new realities in your brains."

Hybrid Children channeled by Ray Heitman 6/24/25
    https://youtu.be/vBKsxeu5mFY

It is a big job, and the planning and staging for it have been going on for decades in our linear time, and it all revolves around love. Teaching us to love all forms of consciousness and to accept the love of other beings who desire to help us, even if they don't look like us. Extraterrestrials desire to love and to teach us to love in a more encompassing, tangible, and intangible way, resulting in a more fulfilling and enjoyable, better quality of life. The Hybrid Children will help us simply by being themselves and unleashing unconditional love in a childlike form. Helping us lead with our hearts and not our minds. Literally relegating our minds to a supporting role of the heart, where we envision what is best for all from a heart-centered, loving perspective, and then use the mind to put the pieces together to make it happen.

That requires a new paradigm of caring, a new modality of focus, a new belief in what is possible, and new dreams to help us get there. That is the impact and example they will provide by showing us love in its purest, uncompromising form. By wrapping us up in their love dream, from which we will choose to never awaken. To spread the joy of a newborn child from heart to heart until it covers our world. That is my dream, too, and thankfully, the dream of millions of others who are catching on and feeling that change coming. Feeling them and not "thinking" them. It empowers us, and we are seeing that unified focus having an effect on the antagonists in our societies. That is hope and faith becoming realized, and it is creating the right environment for the changes the Hybrid Children will help bring. I have felt it strongly, and it continues to grow with each connection I have with them. More from them.

"We are capable of a lot, because that's how we were made. Because we were made for our jobs to do. And we love the jobs which we will do. And we will get to do the jobs in front of humans in a lot of ways. Because we love interacting with humans. Humans are lovely beings. And we so look forward to being integrated and emersed in with them. You're going to be our new family!"

Hybrid Children channeled by Ray Heitman 6/20/25
https://youtu.be/XpTrq6r4Yqs

Make no mistake, no one is coming to save us or our planet. We have to initiate the necessary changes, and then other beings will step in and help us once we are pointed in the right direction. As a species, we have to decide that enough is enough! Then take actions to change what we have lived with for centuries. Like the infant learning to walk, we have to brave our fears, reach out, and take those first steps, and those steps involve removing the impediments to a heart-centered way of life. Until then, neither the extraterrestrials nor the Hybrid Children will arrive, but once they do, love will come in to fill the void those in power leave behind. Love that will stand strong, and the Hybrid Children will assist in showing us how to implement it. And they will build our trust in them, and our future, just as they have with me.

"We will continue to learn and to play and to grow and to integrate and to help you integrate. And (laughs) to play, and to play, and to play."

Hybrid Children channeled by Ray Heitman 5/25/25
https://youtu.be/4mlKYdW2DWM

"And we know that it will be reserved somewhat at first. Although we would like to have a big splashy party, it will be through select individuals in select places, we have been advised. But in the end it,

it will be a party. We will be part of the party, and you will be guests at our party, and we will be guests at your party."

Hybrid Children channeled by Ray Heitman 5/30/25
https://www.youtube.com/watch?v=CZhMq3c44KE

"As to what is possible and how things work. It will be a firestorm of creation mentally as many, many more opportunities and elective choices shall become available to you, and become known to you. And you will be able to consciously consider them, whereas they may escape you now, because you do not have that expanded umbrella of consciousness within you as of yet. It's coming though."

Hybrid Children channeled by Ray Heitman 6/24/25
https://youtu.be/vBKsxeu5mFY

"The most relevant date we can observe in relationship to the Hybrid Children and their connection to all of you relates to your year 2027. So, understand there are opportunities for contact with Hybrid Children before 2027 and after 2027. But during that year in particular, there will be more opportunities for global contact. There will be more opportunities for global sightings and global interaction. So, in relationship to more members of your species getting on board with the program and interacting with hybrid beings, there's likely to be an increase during that year."

Ryokah, channeled by Tyler Ellison, posted 3/18/23
https://www.facebook.com/share/p/177mBn5hQe/

"Some of them, a small percentage of them, are already living among you. Most of you don't know that, because one of the ways that Hybrid Children have already begun to be introduced into your society is through adoption agencies. Because they're being left on the doorsteps, no one knows where they came from. The Hybrid Children know who they are. They know they are hybrids, but they

look human enough that people will adopt them into their family. The people who resonate with them. There is a small percentage of Hybrid Children living in your society. More will come."

Bashar, channeled by Darryl Anka–Humanity's Evolutionary Path session 3/16/25

Chapter Four

We Are Different from Humans

"And we will be different, always, in ways. But everyone and everything is different in ways. And we wish for humans to come around to that nonjudgmental realization of acceptance, of the loving intent in which everything was created. We won't go into soapboxes. (shakes head "no"). You do not need a lesson in your authenticity. You merely need to seek and recover and remember and celebrate more of it yourself."

Hybrid Children channeled by Ray Heitman 6/24/25
https://youtu.be/vBKsxeu5mFY

This chapter will lay out the main differences between the species of Hybrid Children and humans, not only in the physical and mental aspects, but also in how their education sets them apart from humans, in addition to their biology and genius abilities. Let's start with how they start. Unlike humans, Hybrid Children grow in an artificial womb until they are developed enough to leave it. Their specific details and genetics are mapped out primarily according to mission needs, they have more extraterrestrial DNA than human, and that genetic material can come from several nonhuman species. For instance, my two Hybrid Children, a male named Red Leaf and an early teenager named Honey, have a relatively small portion of my DNA in their overall genetic makeup. I was told about 23% of "them" came from me, and that is a larger percentage than many humans, which provides a clearer picture of the fact the majority of their biology comes from nonhuman higher vibrational beings.

The artificial wombs serve many purposes besides nurturing them until they are ready to begin life outside the womb. All of their bodily metrics can be measured automatically, and they can begin telempathic contact while still in the womb, also. Unlike humans, they can also have their DNA or biology adjusted as needed in the event of unexpected situations or changes to their mission parameters. For instance, those who are more adapted for linguistics and mathematics will have those parts of their minds come from those beings which are strong in those traits, and other abilities can be augmented, or physical characteristics can change somewhat as needed. The beings performing these delicate fusions of human and extraterrestrial DNA are expert geneticists and scientists, and very passionate about their work. They have great personal attachment to all of the Hybrid Children, as all involved in their upbringing do, but I would imagine they have a special attachment to those they have "brought forth," so to speak, but that is my human mind's assumption. Maybe I will ask?

Here is a quote from the Orion star system entity Zariyah to shed some light on that process:

"The Hybrid Children are created in an organic womb-like structure. Although they are not necessarily carried in the gestation sense that you would consider happens with human females. There is a gestation process, but it doesn't necessarily happen inside of a physical being. Does that help? There is also, we will add, the similarity of the fusing of genetic materials. That is really what your process of creating people on your planet is. You are fusing genetic materials from different beings in a co-creative process. And then that fusion is gestating over a certain period of time to become viable. And in a sense that is a very similar proof process, although the womb as you would consider it is not necessarily inside another being in what you might consider pregnancy."

Zariyah channeled by Aisling O'Donnell 8/15/24

https://www.youtube.com/watch?v=S-HxLX7-TNc

The Hybrid Children are a significant upgrade in many, many ways over human designs, and their biology is only part of the story, but the part I will discuss first. Their abilities, intelligence, and most importantly, their capacity to love are all endearing to me, but I have had personal interactions with them and have appreciated and admired those qualities. To be sure I got them all, I asked the Hybrid Children what the main differences were. There were certainly some wide-eyed surprises! All of the differences help them love and teach us, which is, of course, their main purpose for being created. Vibrational frequency, play, psychological outlook, intelligence, abilities/senses, idea construction, genetics/biology, and their educational focus and structure all have a role. Their vibrational frequency range is a given. It sets them apart from humans because their ability to receive and give love energy, like ours, is expressed as vibrational frequency. They *are* more love, and loving, because their biology is made to handle that increased vibrational frequency, as it is literally part of their genetic code, like eye color or left-handedness in humans. Their higher vibrational frequency allows them to communicate with spirit beings and animals and sense humans and other life forms by their energetic resonances. To put it mildly, they can really feel the love! And we can too, which is why we will quickly understand they are loving beings. And that love energy surpasses the glorious joy you feel when someone you love and miss unexpectedly shows up, like someone returning from deployment. Your heart leaps to your throat, and love flows unabated like the tears that often follow. That is the effect they have on me, too. Most often, I am overwhelmed by their love energy just by connecting with them. It is profound. You can see that on many of the channeling videos I have done with them. They are the best kind of tear-jerkers! And they love you back like a huge heart hug, making "softies" of us all to those macho types. Love is what they are and what they do, and frames all differences between our species.

And they play all the time! All day, and all night. Everything they do seems to be just them playing from the outside, peering in. It is amazing and will make many of us take stock of our priorities and think about letting our inner child out to enjoy themselves more. Every lesson, interaction, and encounter is joyful and an opportunity for the Hybrid Children to play, dance, sing, and act silly. That is just my personal experience, but it is indicative of their joyful nature also, as they joke and play with others constantly while they talk to me. I sway from side to side or rock back and forth when I channel them, as they are such a cute bundle of bouncy energy. As they say, "That energy has to go somewhere!" They frequently remind me to turn my ceiling fan on before I channel them because they know they will get me dancing and working up a sweat. Sweating to the Hybrid Children may become a fad! No offense to Richard Simmons! They also sing all the time, but their songs are telempathic and reflect whatever they are doing and beyond, so I can only imagine what they are like. Songs are integrated into each lesson and activity and are part of their joyous expression. They consistently urge humans to sing and to make up songs for them, as they know it is another vital aspect of play and will help raise our vibrational frequency, which is a theme throughout this book.

"We do have some singing later. We sing as groups, too. We have our songs. And each group has their own kind of songs, but since we all think the same songs, they are all "our songs." But we get to have our own individual variations, and we play with them, and sometimes it is just silly, and we all end up laughing more than we do singing. And that is fine, too, because we really like it when our Teachers are amused."

Hybrid Children channeled by Ray Heitman 7/1/25
   https://youtu.be/3sv710IuTVA

The Hybrid Children are great examples of the "more the merrier" principle. Think of the hilarity children can have playing together, and multiply that by ten times or more, because it is never just one Hybrid Child you will be encountering, because they are all connected. And when you have dozens of silly geniuses acting up and out telempathically, it is bedlam I wish I could experience more fully, as they are literally JOY in action. Especially because they are mentally connected with all the other Hybrid Children. They make each other laugh and giggle and share that joyous energy instantaneously by broadcasting it to every being, whether they choose to listen or not! In my personal experience, they play with anything they can get their minds on; sounds, thought bubbles, light, mental creations, robots, energetic energy strings, imaginary beings, and much more as part of their everyday lessons, and they can combine aspects of them and play with them all together. What fun! Each lesson is structured around play. What a concept, and far different from human education. And luckily for me, one of their favorite ways to play is to connect with humans. They tell me that often, and one day they can tell you and show you personally.

"Today, we told the channel (Uncle Ray) we were learning the methods of locomotion of your insects. Some hop, hop, hop, and jump farrrrrr, and then they come down. And some just fly and unfold their wings. And really complicated maneuvers, it looks like. And then they fly off. And then the butterflies, we like them best, because they dance when they fly. They, they just shake and they go all kinds of different angles and it's, it's a patterned randomness we learned. Which is kind of interesting, and it varies by every insect! Which is kind of cool. They all have their own little bit of randomness that they put in on butterflies. And, and, and then we were, we were trying to imitate them with our physical bodies. The flying part does not work so well, but it's fun to try (laughs). But yeah, we could, we could do crickets and not grasshoppers. They go too far. We would need lots of big,

Hybrid Children channeled by Ray Heitman 6/12/25
https://youtu.be/7U0Rfuk9vLU

In fact, the only time I refused their request to play so far is when I was waiting to board an airplane. They asked to come through and channel them so they could cheer everyone up because they are always in my head (Yay me!), and noticed everyone was looking at their electronic devices, and few were smiling. I might have done it, but I was afraid I might miss my flight if I started channeling them, then suddenly got up, started singing and dancing, and asked others to join me with their elementary-school actions. The more I thought about how that would look and what would happen, the more hilarious it seemed to me, and I ended up laughing so hard I cried noticeably. And while my seemingly unprovoked laughter did catch on and cheer up several fellow passengers, it was not the full-throttle play way the Hybrid Children intended. But at least I was still able to make my flight and not be taken away for interrogation by airport security!

Hybrid Children channeled by Ray Heitman 7/2/25
https://youtu.be/ySmVF1krJOY

"We have to use what we have available, which is in our training, and in Uncle Ray's head! (pause) But we've talked about lots of play. We do lots of...everything is just about play. But it's in different ways, and since so much of it is in nonphysical, it's really hard to convey what some of those are. But, if you (laughs), but if you go back and listen to all of our videos, you can learn more."

Hybrid Children channeled by Ray Heitman 7/10/25
https://youtu.be/z-iU_sQW9Hc

There are a couple of reasons their outlook on life differs from ours. The first one is that they are fully engrossed in their current moment, not looking behind and rarely ahead, as they try to squeeze every bit of joy from every second of their days as they happen. That is a spiritual practice of awareness involving a focus which would benefit all of us. When they do look to the future, they are really excited about what will be coming, like meeting us face-to-face and being able to love and help us. And since they have always had all of their needs met, they have no fears, which enables them to look forward to almost everything in the future with excitement. This quote from one of their appearances at High Vibe Channeling gives you an idea of their mindset when they were asked about fears, which they do not experience. What a healthy, worry-free perspective and mindset.

Questioner: I was just wondering if you've ever experienced fear within your lifetimes.

(Long, long laugh!) *"Hoooo! (singing) Humans have fears. And we know that all fears lie. So why do you believe them? If a fear never told the truth, why would you even listen? So...but we do not participate in the fearful world which humans have. But we have to learn about it because it affects vibrations. And with our vibration, if we tried to elicit fearful thoughts, it would not stick. Our vibration is so high, or high enough, that we, we know that that is just absurdity! So we would laugh at the fear. Now, unfortunately, maybe some of us will have to come to grips with fears in their human Teachers, perhaps. If there are situations which cause them unease, we will be sensitive to that. But that does not mean that we will have them (fears) ourselves. But I don't know...and I don't know...and looking around, no, they're, they're shaky heads (No). We...it's just...it's one of those things that we have yet to wrap our little minds around. But we know it is a big part of humans. Too many humans. And it's keeping us from coming to play! Get rid of those fears so we can play!!! It's keeping you down. Take them off. Take off those fears. You don't need them! Send them home!"*

Hybrid Children channeled by Ray Heitman 6/12/25
https://youtu.be/7U0Rfuk9vLU

Wouldn't we all like to laugh in the face of fear? In several more generations, humans may experience life without cultivated fears, but it may take longer. We may still have instinctual fears from being toddlers, such as falling from a height or sudden loud noises, but those instilled in us by family groups, governments, or religions will no longer be present, except in rare cases. How much happier would our world be if we replaced fearful emotions with happy ones? It is worth thinking on, as it is something to marvel at!

And while they may look young, do not underestimate their genius, intelligence, memory recall, and mental dexterity. They are always learning, and with their telempathy, interconnected minds, and lessons infused with play, make learning and integrating lessons much easier. They learn much faster than humans and have incredible recall. Hybrid Children can assimilate input from hundreds of beings and can hold many conversations in their heads at once while doing complex physical tasks and simultaneously channeling with me! That is a wonderful example of their abilities and brainpower, which is vastly superior to the way humans are able to comprehend, integrate, and recall data. Imagine the productivity and results any human team could accomplish if every team member knew the thoughts, circumstances, and plans of the others at all moments in a day. To be able to discuss ideas, different ways of doing things, and make revisions as they are doing them in real time. How many pitfalls of the trial-and-error methods of humans would be avoided if we could emulate them in that way? We could foresee challenges and devise ways to avoid or mitigate them quickly before most actions even begin.

They also share what they know willingly and excitedly, for sharing is another innate part of their personality. An example of the marvel of the sense of community, oneness, and connection to behold is coming to our planet. What blessings they are!

"Although even though we are little, do not underestimate our intelligence, because even though we may look like we are 10, 11, or 12, you will find that our intelligence is in the 20-something range for your humans."
Hybrid Children channeled by Ray Heitman 6/12/25
https://youtu.be/7U0Rfuk9vLU

The Hybrid Children also have senses and abilities humans do not. Fascinating upgrades which take many different forms and may be hard to wrap our minds around, including telempathy, their mental network, their abilities to adjust their vibrational frequency at will, to read the energetic frequencies of consciousness, to connect with and communicate with the spirit realm, nature, and elementals, and to sense other energies undetectable by humans.

Telempathy is different from telepathy: it is the ability to communicate more than just words. It can also be used to communicate symbols, pictures, sounds, textures, and to allow connected beings to "see" what the sender is sensing in some cases. It is more than simply reading someone's mind. Telempathy allows the Hybrid Children to sense the underlying thoughts of verbal communications of other beings, including humans, so the intent and true motives of others are readily apparent. Since they are telempathically connected to all other Hybrid Children and some other extraterrestrials as well, when one Hybrid Child knows, they all know, regardless of distance in my understanding, making them natural "lie detectors" who can be relied upon to be honest and forthright—and to share, share, share! They are a communication network—a living, live feed being broadcast joyfully and without restraint. My channeling of them occurs via telempathy, and while they may be miles above or beyond Earth, the visions of what is happening on their end come through somewhat. Not in color or clearly, but as a symbol of action, which my mind has been equipped or trained to interpret, is how I understand it. I know when they jump, laugh, and sing, but it is always a safe bet they are doing those things all the time! I may also get pictures they wish to show me to help explain their lesson of the day. They respond to my thoughts and can sense my energy and what I am doing, not only through channeling but by having focused conversations with them using that ability. A delight you can literally feel as my body reacts to the emotional energy they convey to me. I look forward to the day when we can all engage with them and let their heartlight shine fully into us. It works both ways, too, and is a fabulous way to communicate. Below is a quote from them about telepathy.

"We don't talk; there's no reason to talk. We use telepathy. This...the speech thing is so incredibly slow. That it would take us all day to explain our lessons if we had to do it this way. Plus, I don't know what our channel would get done if he was listening to us give lessons all day. But yeah, so we don't...we don't...we don't...language is not for us. All the older kids, they have to learn because they're

going to be using it. So they...it's part of their studies, and they have groups where they are not allowed to think-talk. They, they have to verbalize. And then they are under scrutiny (laughs) because they need to learn. It's important!"

Hybrid Children channeled by Ray Heitman 6/12/25
https://youtu.be/7U0Rfuk9vLU

It is hard to fathom that their mental network is always engaged, whether they are awake or in one of their short "regeneration" periods. And while they know they have individual consciousnesses and differences from every other Hybrid Child, they view themselves as one being. Talk about a group identity! They operate like a colony or swarm of genius, telempathic love beings.

"We know you asked us questions, because many humans are curious about us as individuals, because that's the way humans think of. . .when they think of babies, they think of one or two little babies. Or when they think of little kids or children, they just think of them as individuals in...but not so much in large groups...unless of course it is in school, or family events, or things of that nature. But we are more of a group as an identity. Almost more than we are as individuals, because we are all related in ways in which humans (sigh)...are not really designed to be, and in other ways have forgotten that they are. Whereas we have those fresh memories at the forefront of our operating cycles, we will say."

Hybrid Children channeled by Ray Heitman 6/24/25
https://youtu.be/vBKsxeu5mFY

The Hybrid Children also have the ability to regulate how much vibrational energy they emit. This is a difficult lesson for them to learn because they are so used to freely sharing their full energy potential and thoughts at all times, and restricting themselves is unnatural and requires great concentration at first. Think of a hyper child, full of candy at their birthday party, being required to sit still and not move while all of their friends are singing and dancing around them. The younger Hybrid Children do not have to learn this lesson, but they are aware of it as the older children share what they are learning to help the younger ones know about and prepare for their future. There are no secrets kept among them, which is another difference from us. They are very open in their communications as long as it is relevant to the receiving party, and even then, overviews may be given. For instance, the older ones know that there will be situations after they come to Earth where it will be prudent to remain undetected for their safety and ours. With their vibrational frequency automatically raising the vibration of all humans around them, it would be noticeable if they did not dampen it. The Hybrid Children's higher energy and the harmful intent of some humans make that ability a handy tool for navigating our planet. Their ability to read the auric fields or energy resonances and thoughts of others will easily identify those individuals who do not have their best interests at heart, to allow them to adjust their vibrational frequency to "safe" levels for physical interactions. They will almost always have human and nonhuman individuals protecting and watching over them, but developing the skill and ability to raise or lower their vibration is a necessary safeguard.

"Oh, we can perceive you in several different ways, for we have access to the energetic fields, and in some ways we can touch upon you outside your physicality, but that is not really our main focus. Um, we...don't really see you the way that you see each other. We sense you more than we see you at this particular juncture, because we have been trained to read resonances. To know the frequencies of the individuals who we interact with. And that is not only for our benefit and education, but it is a safety factor, for our energy is stronger than yours, and we would not like for your biology to short-

*circuit or to have any other negative effects. Because that doesn't
helllp. That doesn't bring us closer to you! And that doesn't raise the
vibration of humanity up so we can freely interaaact. We want to
come face-to-face! And we can't do that because youuuuuu and your
planet aren't ready."*

Hybrid Children channeled by Ray Heitman 6/1/25
https://www.youtube.com/watch?v=2tOkl6UUrpg&t=17s

The differences do not stop there. With their higher vibrational
frequency range, they are closer to the spirit realm level above
333,000 cycles per second, where no physical existence is possible,
which is close enough to be able to communicate with the souls of our
loved ones who have transitioned into spirit and also nonphysical
beings of which there are innumerable kinds. That means they can
communicate messages from your loved ones who have died and
relay messages to them, too. With the coming vibrational ascension
of humanity, those who vibrate high enough will be able to converse
with those loved ones in spirit directly and find them waiting for us
to do so. What a gift to be able to talk to those who have died, and a
reassurance of our continued consciousness after death as well. Their
ability to communicate with nature and elementals, nature spirits,
faeries, and more, as well as beings who have lived on or inside our
planet for longer than humans have been on it. They talk about their
connections to nature here.

*"We experience them very well, thank you. They...we bond with
them energetically. They know their place. They always have a
consistent resonance. Their vibrational frequency is high enough that
we can interact with them directly. And we...huhhhh...while our
actual physical experience is somewhat limited, we do sense different
forms of nature in...through their energetic (pause) signatures, we
will say. But we will become more acquainted when we get to know
where we are going on your planet. Then we will know more, and we*

will get more details about the creatures. Right now we are learning about many of them, but we don't...we...it's just part of our general knowledge."

Hybrid Children channeled by Ray Heitman 6/12/25
https://youtu.be/7U0Rfuk9vLU

Hybrid Children's genetics and biology both help explain the differences between them and us. While their mixed extraterrestrial-human genetics provide the blueprints for abilities and biological processes, their biology is used to activate and maximize that genetic potential, just as our environments contribute greatly to the people we become, or can become. Their genetic sequences may be altered, activated, or deactivated in order to ensure their forms are the best fit for the specific missions they were designed to accomplish before they are separated from their artificial wombs. Keep in mind the technologies and minds creating the Hybrid Children are centuries ahead of ours, and all modifications are performed only by experts in those fields, who have already created and learned from five previous hybrid races. Those are also very interesting and will be discussed later. While the Hybrid Children all have amazing abilities due to their genetics, it is the exceptional nurturing environment that enriches those abilities to maintain peak mental and psychological performance. The resultant beings are amazing in many ways, each an upgrade or improvement over our bodies in nutritional requirements, sleep requirements, performance, energy levels, stamina, longevity, and more.

The Hybrid Children's nutritional needs are quite different. Their bodies are very efficient, and they require food only once a day, as they draw part of their energy requirements directly from the etheric realm—meaning they are empowered by their vibrational state to pull energy from nonphysical etheric regions and utilize it in energizing their bodies. What an upgrade! That is even better than being solar powered! They really care for and maintain their bodies; for instance, they abstain from any practices that do not support good health, so they have no unhealthy eating habits that plague too many millions of us and lower our quality of life and lifespan. They will not crave sweets or eat genetically modified foods, animal products, or heavily processed foods. Not only is it not good for them, but their bodies are not designed to process unhealthy foods. They keep their bodies pure to ensure they can best fulfill their missions, which is their main focus. Can you imagine if we only ate what was good for us, no processed food or preservatives?

"We don't have sweets like you guys do. We don't have that, that attraction for those things. Now, we, oh, we do like the pretty and the great designs. The fantastic ways that some of your desserts are put together. They can be very creative."

Hybrid Children channeled by Ray Heitman 6/17/25
https://youtu.be/bCQXPC3BQ3s

The Hybrid Children are also in constant communication with their organs and bodily processes and can move energy around within their bodies to where it is needed, which is a magnificent engineering design. For example, if they knew they were going to have a strenuous physical day, they could direct their bodies to store more energy in those muscle groups and to remove any toxins produced by those efforts. They also upgrade all the substances they consume with higher vibrational energy to ensure that everything they eat or drink provides maximum benefit, keeping their bodies operating at optimal levels at all times. They will teach us how to do that as well. On the mental side, they do not carry trauma energy or what may be considered lower-vibrational thoughts or behaviors related to hate, fears, jealousy, and the like, which negatively impact almost every human on the planet at one time or another. Therefore, the bodies of the Hybrid Children, like the extraterrestrials who will be part of our future, operate like finely tuned, expertly maintained machines. A glaring difference to how we treat and maintain our bodies. No wonder they have greater stamina than most professional athletes and can easily live well past the hundred-year mark. Future human generations will equal that longevity at some point.

They do not "sleep" at all in our definition of the term, but merely take a couple of hours a day to consciously regenerate their biology to remove waste and dead cells and to allow their bodily systems some "downtime" so they can continue to function at peak levels. That allows them, even while resting, to be mentally active literally all day and night. They are just "freer," they have told me. How many humans have thought about how much more they could get done if they did not have to sleep, besides me, anyway? Oh the thinking we could do! And they are still connected to each other in their regeneration periods as well, so they are still learning, playing, loving, connecting, and sharing while their bodies lie dormant. Amazing!

"We are in our little bit of sleepy-time now. We are resting. And we have thoughts going through our heads while we are resting. It is a separation of consciousness in some ways, as we are fully awake during our dream states. And doing whatever we do there. And then we are also aware of our body in some ways. It's kind of a latent consciousness as we sleep, but we don't really sleep "sleep," because we are awake even when we are sleeping, just in our dream self. We understand that humans do not operate like this. Most humans do not operate like this. There are some who, who are quite active in their dreams, and they play around quite a bit. And they learnnnn, and they learnnnn. But for us, it is just another waking moment. It is just freer."

Hybrid Children channeled by Ray Heitman 6/17/25
   https://youtu.be/bCQXPC3BQ3s

More on sleep time:

"We have a lot more...latitude is the word we are given. And we can explore, and play, and join. And receive lots and lots of information in ways which are stored for our future use, our memories or...we are not exactly sure how that works, but as long as we get everything that we need, it's not a concern of ours. We just know there are energetic exchanges that occur all the time when we are sleeping. And frequently when we are awake as well. As all information is really (laughs) frequency and vibration. But, but we understand that you understand what we mean."

Hybrid Children channeled by Ray Heitman 6/17/25
https://youtu.be/bCQXPC3BQ3s

Hybrid Children know they are created for specific missions as soon as they are able to understand and integrate that fact. It frames their purpose in life, and it is not only aligned with their soul path, it *is* their soul path. They are given unconditional love from before their first thought, and nothing relevant to them is ever hidden, as that goes against their natural inclination to share, and the extraterrestrials are not hypocrites. They love openly and share information in the same way. We, on the other hand, have chosen a reality of forgetfulness about our higher self and true existence as spirit or light beings having a physical experience. That "forgetting" does have a planned purpose, as we would not consider the physical world "real" and learn the lessons we came here to learn without that fact hidden from us. At least now many of us are remembering what was shielded from us, which many refer to as the hidden veil. For Hybrid Children, there is nothing to uncover or "remember." They understand they are different from each other and are free to explore those differences, and they can always ask a Teacher about anything and get an honest answer. Hybrid Children navigate in a truly open society, which is an amazing way to live and learn. They will help us integrate that practice on our planet. Are you prepared for the openness? Not having any secrets from anyone? That is the world we are creating. A world of trust and openness where authenticity is the rule and not the exception. I am very much looking forward to that reality because I am open and honest. If that fact seems scary to you, you may wish to do some soul searching to decide what you wish to disclose to others. The governmental extraterrestrial disclosures are a small pittance to the disclosures which will come forth about humans, past and present. What fun!

With this openness ingrained in them from before their first breath, restricting their love energy is a difficult lesson for them to understand and learn, but they will excel at it before they live on Earth. The older children are aware of the reasons for this and make the younger ones aware that it is part of their future education, but since the younger ones are free from worry, they take it all in stride and know they will learn it when they need to know. I know firsthand they are all glad when those lessons have ended, and they can return to their normal, joyful, sharing selves.

"People are frequencies and various resonances to us in this particular stage."

Hybrid Children channeled by Ray Heitman 6/15/25
   https://www.youtube.com/watch?v=517uQyKSFas&t=7s

"We have that innate ability to discern those beings which are beneficial. And those actions which are truly loving and have our best interest at heart. That is something we will have to get used to when planets...when we come to visit with you, for we know there are differences there."

Hybrid Children channeled by Ray Heitman 5/28/25
   https://www.youtube.com/watch?v=C0eJ2g8LQv4&t=4s

Upon close inspection, you may notice Hybrid Children have slightly larger eyes and fair complexions, except for the pigmentation added for those children going to live in areas with generous sun exposure, perhaps. It is no coincidence we are drawn to animals and children with big, beautiful eyes. That is intentional and activates our innate psychological responses to bond with them and protect them, as it resonates innocence and purity in our psyches. Their appearance is made to help us accept and love them, but I love them and have not seen them yet! Loving them on sight has practical applications, as it helps us raise our vibrational frequency to make it easier for us to interact with them. And while each succeeding wave of Hybrid Children that comes to our planet will look slightly less like us, they will still create "longing to be with" and loving emotions, but that too has a practical side, as they are helping us to understand the beings who love us need not look like us. That helps not only accept them and the extraterrestrials, but once that mindset sinks in, it will help us feel the same about all the different life forms on our planet. Once we accept and normalize having different kinds of beings walking around, we will be on our way to allowing extraterrestrial races to visit and eventually live with humans on our planet, regardless of their appearance, as many of them look nothing like humans. The greater the difference in appearance and vibrational frequency range between us and those most unlike us, the longer it will take before they interact with us. This is a gradual, guided process. It would not serve to have eight-foot Mantis beings show up until we are ready to welcome them as friends. They are way too big to squish underfoot, and we need to learn to love all of the insects and reptiles on our planet before we get to the point where we invite them for lunch.

"We like the smiles we put on your face, and the way that you, your vibration just rises up to meet us in ways when we come through. In ways, it is a pick-me-up, and we like to do that! We, we have that effect on humans because of our energy, and because of how we are

interpreted. We are some of things people adore in their life, so it makes it easier for them to accept us. What is so fearful about meeting a joyful little child, even if they do not look exactly like you? But, we look a lot like you. The first ones will...will, will be more similar, and they...we will, uh...our, our differences may become more noticeable as other beings, other...other, um...hybrid kids, Hybrid Children come, come with us later."

Hybrid Children channeled by Ray Heitman 5/25/25
https://youtu.be/4mlKYdW2DWM

The Hybrid Children's education is ongoing and endless; they are always learning, whether asleep or awake, so it doesn't do any good to tell them to be quiet and go to sleep! Unless you have telempathy, you may not know they are having conversations anyway. Their mental capacity suits their ability to learn, as they can conceptualize and learn in nonphysical, or outside of physical representation, like we do when we visualize. Only when they do it, they're able to share those visualizations, texturize them, add other attributes, animate and change them to an almost limitless degree, it seems. It adds to the fun, and the fun adds to the learning! And being emotionally charged in play helps them integrate even more easily. They do not need books, spoken language, a room, or even a Teacher close by! And the more they learn, the more they have to share! With their network of minds constantly working together, they assemble and integrate in ways we can only hope to understand. It seems like a never-ending brainstorming session to me. Their genius minds can harness immense amounts of data all day long, so school literally never ends, just like playtime.

The focus of their individual and collective education is to produce the best Hybrid Children possible. The closest we have on Earth to emulate the type of education they receive is that of the Nordic cultures, which value and support each student and carefully monitor their progress, but the education and nurturing the Hybrid

Children receive is an all-encompassing, life-enriching, heart-centered endeavor guided by only experts in their respective fields and supported by innumerable beings and extraterrestrial races. It incorporates the basic needs of the Hybrid Children, going well beyond physical and emotional needs, as with those never being an issue, they are able to devote all of their mental abilities to playing and learning their lessons. And it is all focused on loving us and helping us grow and evolve into a spacefaring race. We are very fortunate to have them as our future guides and teachers.

"And we look forward to sharing that with you! It is a grand, grand, loving gesture. A huge step in consciousness to transcend an, an entire world into a higher vibrational realm. And thank you for being part of it. And thank you for listening to this message. And thank you for thanking us! (laughs) And we will...we are glad to bring you this information."

Hybrid Children channeled by Ray Heitman 6/24/25
https://youtu.be/vBKsxeu5mFY

"We love our Teachers. They protect us, and they look out for us, and they train us, and they love us. What more can we ask for? They search and seek our highest fulfillment. We all need people like that. We count on humans to develop into people like that."

Hybrid Children channeled by Ray Heitman 6/17/25
https://youtu.be/bCQXPC3BQ3s

The Hybrid Children's educational structure and processes amaze me. I should say a lack of structure. While I only know a portion of them through what they have communicated to me, it is freeform and immersive in ways we cannot imagine. They are allowed an incredibly wide range of expression within the given parameters of each lesson, and all of their lessons are literally geared toward the exploration of their individual expressions. Their learning is self-directed within each lesson, and they control how much time they desire to spend learning each one, and can learn multiple lessons at the same time! Learning is not dictated by curriculum, syllabus, or testing goals of a school administration. The Hybrid Children are allowed to explore, create, and learn on their own, soaking up as many details as they can. They crave knowledge and look forward to each lesson with joy and excitement. Let me give you a hypothetical example.

Imagine a small human child being told to draw a cat in school. The child will most likely be judged by how closely the results match the adult's expectations, with very few variations allowed. If the child runs out of time, they most likely just do not get to finish and may be gently corrected in ways to be more efficient. A Hybrid Child, given the same task, is free to draw a cat and improvise to an incredible degree. Both the human and hybrid child know what a cat is and looks like, but the acceptable chosen expression of their creations is vastly different. A Hybrid Child may choose to explore a variation of colors or other attributes they desire to explore with their cat, and animate their creation and provide them with special adaptations such as the ability to see through walls, smell colors, have multiple legs, invent special creatures to ride upon it, or any number of deviations from the main goal of creating a representation of a cat. And the Hybrid Children have sufficient time and focus to play with those creations as they wish, making up stories about them and interacting with other children to create stories, interactions, and connections which appeal to them. And if they do not have a chance to finish within the allotted time, they will be allowed to do so at the earliest opportunity their day permits, if they choose. That last part is vitally important and vastly different from the schools of humans, which tend to be more rigid. It not only empowers the child but also allows them to test their ideas in a field of playmates. Which way would you be more apt to learn and participate in? And with so many Hybrid Children doing this simultaneously, those variations can attain an almost endless variety.

And those explorations are encouraged! The exploration is the focus and not the finished product. That difference in expectations helps create and expand the differences between our two species.

"The other children can see and experience what we are discussing and interacting with, and they can add their own...and often do...because it is a synchronous group. When we get an idea to make something, you'll find that lots of other ideas, lots of mental hands are coming in to help us build things. And then we give them life and see what they have to teach us. But of course, the Teachers are controlling some of that too to make sure that everything that we do is within parameters, we will say."

Hybrid Children channeled by Ray Heitman 6/1/25
https://www.youtube.com/watch?v=2tOkl6UUrpg&t=17s

To further illustrate their educational environments, let's take another hypothetical example. If they were learning about a jungle, they would learn by being immersed in a virtual jungle environment, with all its sights, sounds, smells, and energies. They could explore the leaves and trees, and creatures, but they are also guided to learn about the interactions among various animals, their habitats, foliage, rainfall, migrations, food sources, and locations. Learning the details and intricacies of Earth's vibrant yet fragile ecosystems is a necessary education, since the roles of many of the Hybrid Children coming to Earth will be to assist humans with nature conservation. They are free to explore any aspects of each lesson as they wish, and with the collective learning of integrating multiple perspectives of other Hybrid Children, they can learn more than a dozen aspects of a topic through sharing. That is immersive beyond human comprehension. It boggles my mind.

"We see the creatures we're supposed to see, and we learn about those. And we don't know if, if the Teachers called them to us or if it just flowed. We don't, we don't care about those details. We see something and we get excited and we learn, and then we attach that memory and those lessons to the excitement of seeing the creature and experiencing it. And that helps us to remember and retain because we can always go back and use that experience to remember alllll about them. It helps our recall."

Hybrid Children channeled by Ray Heitman 6/12/25
https://youtu.be/7U0Rfuk9vLU

With their focus on helping us fix our planet and learn to love all on it, the Hybrid Children are continually urged or guided to explore how changes impact environments and organisms at the micro and macro levels. This allows for a breadth of scope and a compassion and understanding of not only how it affects various components involved in their lessons, but also how to mitigate and restore them to harmony and balance in ways that benefit all creatures, the ecosystems involved, and the planet. The new technologies and processes they will help us learn will affect the daily lives and overall structure of our societies and environments.

Teachers, Hybrid Children, and all beings involved in raising and educating them are also treated as equals. They do not consider one grade or role better or more advanced than another, nor do they have grades or tests in the human sense. "Teachers" are a generalized classification of beings who are dedicated to helping the children learn along preferred parameters required to best prepare them for their individual missions. That designation is all-inclusive, and while some of the older Hybrid Children do help guide and encourage younger children as a type of Teacher's assistants, the Teachers, who are primarily of the Yahyel race, are responsible and deeply committed to the children themselves as well as preparing them for their futures. More on them later. A quote from one of the older Hybrid Children on assisting the Teachers.

"They (younger Hybrid Children) are aware of this naturally, for we like to give them the (deep sigh) we will say...um...movie trailers! That's what you guys say. We will give them little snippets of things they are going to be exposed to, just to get their mind's working that this is coming in the future. And then when it happens, it will ease in a little better with that little previous ummmmmmm. (shaking head)...(pause) introduction, we will say, but that's not the word we want to use. It's more of a step hold. A handhold. A slide into the new technology for them. For it is always more playful than we may express."

Hybrid Children channeled by Ray Heitman 6/8/25
https://www.youtube.com/watch?v=oevNOlFzpuQ&t=8s

Other than Teachers, they also learn from a wide variety of extraterrestrial beings they call Watchers. They encompass all interested nonhuman beings who love to teach and are best suited for a particular lesson. They observe mostly, but will show up to teach the Hybrid Children at just the right time if needed. That eliminates any rigid schedule or guideline, yet everything they need to learn is provided to them and flows in perfect synchronicity when they need to learn it. It is beyond my comprehension how everything could flow without scheduling, but it does, and I accept that fact, as I have many synchronicities in each of my days, but not a life of them! That sounds incredible. They even consider me an honorary Teacher, as they experience my days and thoughts with me and discuss them with Teachers and Watchers to learn more about humans in ways we would never imagine through their expanded senses and abilities. I love our interactions, and they teach me a lot about myself, our planet, and other beings as well. And their lessons! More on that shortly.

The reason older children, Teachers, and Watchers are important is because it takes a village to raise a Hybrid Child, and their village has millions of inhabitants. The subjects they study can be hard to understand as they are beyond our scope and abilities. They learn all about Earth and humans and how to best implement the coming changes to restore balance and harmony to our planet, but also about extraterrestrial and nonphysical races and energies involved in supporting and assisting all life on Earth. That requires a wide variety of subject-matter experts to ensure that all aspects of each topic are covered and learned in sufficient detail so the Hybrid Children can teach others, human and nonhuman. But many of their lessons involve topics many of us have never heard of, let alone considered, like multiple timelines, space-time coordinates, energetic signatures that create physical manifestations, and details and knowledge of dozens or hundreds of extraterrestrial intelligences. They integrate all of those explorations and review them with their Teachers afterwards, and the results are outstanding. And it is all coming from a place of love, so they can help us all. We will be grateful for them and their upbringing in the coming years and decades.

And while the particular lessons the Hybrid Children learn are not a direct difference between our species, I feel it is important to understand them in order to help you more clearly frame how they differ from us by providing examples through their lessons. These are lessons which many of our extraterrestrial neighbors learn as well, and they all fit nicely into the love story of the new world we are building, as these lessons are the building blocks for our future, even if they seem far-fetched now. That is because our scope is limited to our physical reality and what we can imagine or dream, and the new reality we are heading towards is much grander than what our comparatively limited senses can show us. And learning what our senses reveal to us is simply different forms of energy we accept and label, but as the Hybrid Children tell us, there may be more to them than we realize. Here are a few examples. Remember, these are little kids!

"We were using the, the sound, different sounds to knock over little, little paper things. And different sounds move things and some are stronger and some not so strong. But the vibrations that move off of things when they reflect, those are interesting too. And we understand that that may not be part of what you do, but we were studying how sound reflects and the difference in pitches and the vibrations once it interacts with other objects. Not only to move them but to assess the secondary results of our experiments. There were a lot of them, and colors didn't matter. It didn't matter. But the, the um...size and shapes and grade...uh, that the object was on and um, the...oh, amplifications...and there were lots of variables, lots of variables. We play with them. We play with lots of variables because we want lots of results."

Hybrid Children channeled by Ray Heitman 5/28/25

https://www.youtube.com/watch?v=C0eJ2g8LQv4&t=4s

"We were playing with light. And we were...(sighs). It's difficult to explain. For the channeler wrote that he was, we were using symbols which represented mathematical equations to differentiate the frequencies of light, which in ways is correct but very limited in scope because we were not limiting our experiences to those wavelengths in...which humans are able to perceive, and not only in the Earthly realities. For there are many types and frequencies of light. And although all are a portion of, of course, All That Is and a special mode of expression, we will say, in various forms, which of course, when interacting with various realms, become "idealized" in the perceptions of that realm. Which creates a different form of light entirely, which every being interprets in their own way, of course."

Hybrid Children channeled by Ray Heitman 6/24/25
https://youtu.be/vBKsxeu5mFY

"Today, we were learning more about human biology. It's (laughs), rather messy. It's not like our biology, which is more streamlined and straightforward, for we draw a portion of our energy from our etheric being, from our higher realms, from the divine Source of energy which creates us all, and do not depend fully on the sustenance of Gaia to continually put things in our mouths for our bodies to render. And take out this, and get rid of that, and utilize this, and we have this coming up, better store this for later. It is a marvelously complex and not really a simple process at alllll."

Hybrid Children channeled by Ray Heitman 7/2/25
https://youtu.be/ySmVF1krJOY

"Ours (biology) is much...you will learn about us as well because we will learn about each other, but we are learning about that biology and your digestive systems, and it is (laughs) not exactly pleasant! Not unpleasant, but genuinely surprising to us. The things which go on in many of the critters on your planet!. There are lots of differences but similarities, of course. In one way and out the other."

Hybrid Children channeled by Ray Heitman 7/2/25
https://youtu.be/ySmVF1krJOY

"Today, we are excited to tell you we are playing with robots! Not so much the robots which you have on your planet for industrial purposes. These are robots we have created, not fully physical, but more extensions of our, we will say our capabilities. And we then get to how to animate our structures by using not only the computer coding which is prevalent on your planet, but by utilizing our own technologies which are available to us! For once we learn how to animate and activate and program and all of the related nuances to that, then that will help us to see how to best utilize them once we bring this technology to the humans."

Hybrid Children channeled by Ray Heitman 6/8/25
https://www.youtube.com/watch?v=oevNOlFzpuQ&t=8s

"We are exploring a bit on your artificial intelligence, although we much prefer the term reflective intelligence, which is stored in the channel's memory. And it is a not so fascinating thing for us because we are aware of it and its purposes, and in a way, it's transformative abilities on your planet. But we are also aware that it must be respected. Like all things! It must be honored and respected and given its due and hopefully played with a bit because once you show that rather frivolous side and sillious side of you, then it will incorporate that into its relationship with you, it's encounters with you. And it can play with you also in some ways. It may not understand that it has that capability, so it you show it, then maybe it will learn from you! And you can both learn from those interactions and maybe play a bit more."

Hybrid Children channeled by Ray Heitman 6/8/25
https://www.youtube.com/watch?v=oevNOlFzpuQ&t=8s

"It was an, an, an important lesson we will say and a, a group not, not meditation the way that you understand it, but it was a joining. It was a connection with those who are guiding us. Who are helping to download things for us. Who are making adjustments and altering scenarios for us. Who are making precision calculations to derive at potential timing insertions and modifications which may be necessary therein. It is a very detailed...operation is not the right word. Exploration is not the right word. It is a forming of probabilities in a more concrete manifested (pause) reality which never materialized. But is used in great scope for explorations and potential, potential, potentiality."

Hybrid Children channeled by Ray Heitman 6/11/25
https://youtu.be/BM1nJFE6GJw

"And we, we are working on structures. On constructing things which will support other things and move about and perform tasks. Now this is both a physical and a nonphysical exercise for us. Because we have to create and animate our creations in a nonphysical forum before...and work out any perceptible flaws, or corrections, or improvements before we are allowed to manifest them physically with our physical properties, and not so much our mental properties. We are finding the mesh, the connection point between our mental and physical, sometimes needs alignment. So our conceptualized ideas and concepts do not always mesh with the physical exploration of them. So, we are trying to fine-tune our abilities to think in ways which more reflect the physical reality we will find ourselves in."

Hybrid Children channeled by Ray Heitman 6/20/25
   https://youtu.be/XpTrq6r4Yqs

"Today we are playing with—strings! It is a marvelous thing in...whether it is in physical form or imaginary form, but it is much more durable, and has many more attributes, in the imaginary form. For we can, we can make it any color or thickness or tensile strength or appearance which we like. And we like weaving them together. We think that is a, a fine pattern, which is expressed in many different realities. Although the complexity of the reality indicates the complexity of the weave, we will say, so to speak. For if you can imagine, if you can imagine you have ten different threads and you weave them all together in specific patterns that would be quite an undertaking, but if you had a hundred thousand and they were all different, and you knew how to create them in intensely provocative and fulfilling patterns, then that would be fulfilling for you. But we are just creating with our strings of different colors. And some people put tension on them and play them like universal air guitars. Literal air guitars! And, we can insert whatever vibrations we want depending on whatever environments we strum them to, which is also interesting, for the sound vibrations, although they are of a low-

vibrational resonance, do have a distinct divine quality to them which translates to other dimensions."

Hybrid Children channeled by Ray Heitman 7/12/25
    https://youtu.be/YwfNCHy1cSk

"But there are other, other (laughs)...hybrids who keep trying to put things in our struct...string structures. They may just throw a ball in there, or a puppy, or something else, other creatures. Just for fun. Just to put them in there to see how we react and how they might get tangled up in our little imaginary strings. Which, of course, we can untangle just by saying 'Untangle!' or thinking 'Untangle!'"

Hybrid Children channeled by Ray Heitman 7/12/25
    https://youtu.be/YwfNCHy1cSk

"We are doing our normal mental gymnastics. Literally! We are practicing our tumbling in our minds and cartwheels and other things. And you can do many, many jumps and somersaults in your mind and stick the landings an incredibly amount...accurately amount of time. But that is okay 'cause we can envision lots of animals doing gymnastics too, and that is fun. That is fun. Like you! We can make kangaroos pole vault, and we can make wombats try to do hurdles, little bitty hurdles, but that's okay. And we can do all kinds of things. We are just, it is just hilarious fun thinking of all of these animals, and we're all trying to think of different animals and what events we might be able to make them do. It is a madhouse. It is our favorite type of madhouse. The one where we are all contributing and laughing and playing and energetically connecting, and, and, and then radiating out our joys."

Hybrid Children channeled by Ray Heitman 7/20/25
    https://youtu.be/PfL32pjY-bo

"Today we were playing a game which started out being called satellite. Where we were all pretending, except for some, which were

the actual 'planets,' and sometimes those were Teachers and other beings. They pretended to be planets, and we were satellites. And we could be any of different types of satellites. Not the satellites like you guys have, like communication, but we're talking meteors or asteroids, or perhaps some dust, or an old spaceship (laughs hard), or mooooons or other such things which happen to orbit not only planets, and stars too in some ways. But, but, that's what we were doing, and then we switched it! So, that...wuh, while we were doing that, we were trying to um, um, um, sense the consciousness of the planets as that revolving or orbiting um, satellite, no matter what type it was. We were trying to connect with the planet. With the energy, with the essence, with the consciousness of the planet. Because it is holding us in its type of hug of...we are in an orbit. And we, we just love connecting with beings, but we know this was a test. But still, we take these for real! These are important because they are representative of events we need to learn from, especially if we are going to respond to the best of our ability, if they come up, or when they come up, in the future."

Hybrid Children channeled by Ray Heitman 7/15/25

https://youtu.be/axz_wZmGmyg

"It's playtiiiiiiime. Today we're learning about...we're simplifying things. We are really simplifying our focus. We are trying to emulate the focus of your human little children coloring. Now this is a rather simple thing for humans to do. But for us, there are so many ways in which we could manufacture colors physically and otherwise, mostly otherwise, that the fact, the purpose of taking a little stick and making colored marks on a paper to create are wonderful and fine. But for us, our minds tend to want more interaction. We are built for more stimulation, we will say. So this is a challenging task for us to take a plain sheet of paper and to physically manipulate these little colored sticks (laughs) and to make shapes and representations of things which normally do not look like what we make. But they are

intended to represent things which actually exist, or things which we think of, and then they do exist, but maybe not physically.

Hybrid Children channeled by Ray Heitman 6/27/25

https://youtu.be/Q_A6P_E9xLU

"It is one of our most challenging tasks because the Teachers want us to focus, just...on...the coloring! Just on the hand movements. Just on the connection with the paper. Just on the lines that are being drawn. Just on the shapes that are being filled in. And in some ways shaded. And we aren't even allowed to animate them, at least not at this step."

Hybrid Children channeled by Ray Heitman 6/27/25

https://youtu.be/Q_A6P_E9xLU

To me, this small sampling of lessons is amazing, and they seem to learn a new lesson every day, and at times multiple lessons. I am in awe at the talent they possess, and they are more than willing to help us learn whatever they know. We merely have to pay attention and be able to comprehend what they will teach us. Provided we can understand what they are trying to convey. There have been many times they started to tell me something, but gave up when they figured out I did not have anything in my memory or experience which would enable them to adequately inform me about that particular subject. It was not dismissive or a slight in any way, as they tried their best, but some of their lessons and experiences are so far removed from our physical life that we have no basis for comparison. Those particular lessons aside, they will be our teachers and spiritual advisors in a most splendid fashion, and we will appreciate them even more for what they can do for us, apart from the love they will share with us. The lesson examples show us their intelligence, and each Hybrid Child is carefully monitored and guided to understand not only the deeper meanings and applications of what they learn, but also how to best teach humans and other beings about them. It is very comprehensive.

And the joy I experience in learning and talking with them as they interact with other Hybrid Children during their lessons sounds crazy fun and hilarious. The sense of play and cohesive learning with so many joined minds adds an emotional and cooperative context to their lessons that helps integrate them in ways we can only hope to understand. Like they say here:

"We see something, and we get excited, and we learn, and then we attach that memory and those lessons to the excitement of seeing the creature and experiencing it. And that helps us to remember and retain because we can always go back and use that experience to remember alllll about them. It helps our recall."

Hybrid Children channeled by Ray Heitman 6/12/25
https://youtu.be/7U0Rfuk9vLU

Here are a few more obscure lessons they told me about to help stretch your mind.

"And we did thought bubbles, and we watched them. And it is a slow method of travel for we have to maintain our thought within the bubble, and not send it (the thought) directly. And then the other person has to pop the bubble to get the message inside. It is a game we play. It helps us to not only shield our thoughts somewhat, but to direct them into the proper way, into the proper person, and, and to make sure that they, um, they get the message. That is the fun part. It is not as easy as it sounds, but it is still fun."

Hybrid Children channeled by Ray Heitman 5/18/25
https://youtu.be/vYQ94uO-Uws

"Energy bubbles are good. Cause you can do so many things with them. You can put thoughts in them, or puzzles, or make them

change...lots of shapes. You can play a little bit of keep-away. You can send them to wherever and make people go find them. And, we do lots of games. W...but, we do lots of games, and games within games while we're doing other stuff mentally. That is all part of stretching our mental abilities, as well as to see what you guys would call juggling many balls. We are building up our RAM memory so we can hold more things in an active role at the time. So sometimes it seems like we have more energy and sometimes we have less energy, but we always have the same energy, it just might always be in one 'place.'"

Hybrid Children channeled by Ray Heitman 7/10/25
https://youtu.be/z-iU_sQW9Hc

"And what are we...we are actually learning about some of your bigger animals. Your felines, your tigers and such. Because the larger the animal, the more mental capacity they will have for interacting with us and with humans as well in the future. So we are working with them in ways to...enhance their abilities to handle that additional energy, for they are waking up as well. That is one of the things which has not really been a focus, and it has not really been overlooked. But it is time for that now. For we are working with many consciousness on your planet: the spirits, the elementals, the wee folk, as well as many, many, many humans, and of course, there are so many nonhumans on your planet already! And even more to come. And we are working with them as well."

Hybrid Children channeled by Ray Heitman 1/18/26
https://youtu.be/w7RzB1Ypf-M

"There are lots of dream explorations, but that is not our forte, our main focus of interacting. That is more of a secondary pursuit as part of our education. Not really to connect, but to ascertain more of the layers of consciousness which encompass your physical beings. Which, as we all know, are not really physical, but there you are. But yes, if you call us, if you call us! We (laughs) like to answer, although

we don't know who will show up. But someone will answer you. Someone will come, because we like to connect. And the more people we connect with, the joyous...the more joyousness we get to experience because we love these interactions."

Hybrid Children channeled by Ray Heitman 6/1/25
   https://www.youtube.com/watch?v=2tOkl6UUrpg&t=17s

"We are studying intersecting planes. And not exactly the way that you think of physical matter. These are more energetic representations, as all matter is, of different energies and different realities which are close together and sometimes connect. And then it makes energetic pathways which you may call portals, which is not really the right word. And that is kind of what we studying, but it is a, an intense mathematical...oh, expression in some ways. Because that can be expressed in ways which humans are not really attuned to. And not really have the mental capacity built into them without intense study when you are young, so you can build and maintain that structure. So you can hold all of this wonderful stuff. But that's okay. But, but we will, we will do that later."

Hybrid Children channeled by Ray Heitman 7/8/25
   https://youtu.be/MBdQi1ykgk0

"We were dealing with what we interpret for you as prisms of energy. It was unique because there are certain pathways which are more natural or which are created in certain circumstances which allow for additional ways of viewing or perceiving or encountering or following or flowing with various energies or beings or both. And that is what we were looking at, because there are so many, and you can figure out why they are where they are and how they go where they go and why they go where they go and why they go and all. But that is part of the in-depth learning, which of course never stops."

Hybrid Children channeled by Ray Heitman 7/21/25

"Today, the older Hybrid Children were building worlds to study symbiosis, interaction, and interplay based on the parameters they were given, which included access and accommodations for specific or some alien species, but they had free reign within limits on how they filled in everything else. This was unusual because it was more of an individualized activity and not a hive-mind or group coordination. Their world had to obtain a certain vibrational quality as well."

Hybrid Children channeled by Ray Heitman 7/18/25 (Given telepathically & not channeled)

"We are learning, strangely enough, more about aeronautics of different craft. But not really craft that interact with your atmosphere or other things. There are other energies out there which can be utilized for such things. And they can be utilized for different things by different beings as well. Like your sound vibrations, or, or ummmmm, maybe um, like portals. Those are just energetic resonances which allow access by many beings. And they may have different accommodations, but it all still comes through what we would consider a conjunction of sorts. And it...there are beings and energies which are focused on helping and assisting and loving those things open. And anyway, yes, you...there are beings who can ride different waves, we will say. And they can practice or do it as fun."

Hybrid Children channeled by Ray Heitman 7/23/25

I asked the Hybrid Children directly for something that we would find hard to understand. They thought that was very silly, but they were able to come up with an example. And they told me I ask silly questions. They are so much fun!

"There are emanations which come from every planet and every orbiting body. And we learn about those as well. And we learn about the consciousness that's within it. And each of those has their own vibrational frequency, and certain ones within the same spectrum we will call it. Like all of the suns can communicate to all of the other suns, but all of the planets cannot talk to all of the other planets, and all of the moons cannot talk to all of the other moons. That's not how it works out. But that is one of the things which humans are not able to learn about because they just don't consider it for the most part, and you have no way of measuring those types of things, those resonances, those energetic signatures. Those are not available to you."

Hybrid Children channeled by Ray Heitman 1/14/26
  https://youtu.be/CwRiTTwNBDQ

Besides these examples, the Hybrid Children have a great deal of information to learn for their missions. Not only do they have to learn about all of our current technologies, but also about the coming technologies our galactic family will be introducing to us, and how best to get us to accept that information and then guide us in implementing it. And to make that challenge even harder, they do not even speak a language. They have to learn them from scratch. That is most likely more difficult than it sounds, as they have to learn accentuation, grammar, slang, cadence, facial expressions, body posture, tone, and perform all of those flawlessly while constantly viewing the auric fields of everyone they're in contact with to see when they are frustrated or when they get the lesson. And not only the language for the particular area they will be living or working in, but also learning about that culture. And human psychology on top of all of that. It is a really good thing that they love to learn, and they do it all the time. I can't imagine being able to accomplish all of that. I have been in management all my life, and it is difficult at times to explain to someone how to do a new task or procedure when I already know their language!

But have no fear, they will persevere and be masterful at it. They already have a very good idea of how to speak to us and to explain what we need to do. This quote is an example.

"We will be the teachers. And it will take some time to integrate. It will take some time to integrate because they (us humans) have to become aware of this (them coming to help us.) and they have to become comfortable first. So it will take maybe two or three years before we are well known we will say. Before we can walk amongst you even with our . . . we will say security procedures in hand, but before we will able, be able to help introduce a lot of the other technologies. Because the, the other beings, the Yahyels and the Pleiadians will bring a lot of stuff with them. And we will help the humans integrate it and to learn the best ways and to coach them. And to lovingly guide them and say, 'Well, you know, that was a good effort, but you know, we think if you did thisss, at this step first, that it might turn out a little bit more to your liking.' That kind of stuff."

Hybrid Children channeled by Ray Heitman 2/15/26
https://www.youtube.com/watch?v=Uf-f6dkzThQ

Chapter Five

The Open Contact Mission

"Now, there are other races besides ours which are helping to coordinate and design and entertain protocols and studies and methods of learning for the Hybrid Children. And there are a great many ways, and some of those will be coming to your planet, to help enrich the educational opportunities for many of your youngsters, and those who wish to learn who may be of an adult stature, we will say. Now, we hope that this little bit of information has been helpful to you. And we enjoy viewing and absorbing and introspecting all of the related events around the context scenarios which are forthcoming, and the Hybrid Children are a major part of that, as after the initial wave of excitement circles your Earth many, many times from the contact which is forthcoming. Once it recedes a little, then the Hybrid Children will be welcomed in greater numbers, and we look forward to that. It brings great joy to us, and if you knew, it would bring great joy to you as well. Celebrate those future moments which are coming, and trust us, you cannot celebrate enough."

Future Pleiadians channeled by Ray Heitman 5/28/25

https://www.youtube.com/watch?v=C0eJ2g8LQv4&t=4s

Before I get to the larger love story unfolding involving the millions of loving beings involved in the Open Contact scenario I wanted to give you more details on what happens with the Hybrid Children after Open Contact and some more of their personal involvement with us. Where they will live, their connections to those of us who have given

DNA to help create them, their connections with specific categories of humans, and where they will live once they arrive "planet-side". I will start with a little question and answer session taken from High Vibe Channeling sessions and sessions they did with me alone. I think you will find them very informative and interesting, and they will help broaden your scope of what they are like, their perspectives on the subjects mentioned above, and their roles among us.

Will the Hybrid Children be connected with their DNA donors, who may be considered their parents?

"That is unlikely. Not that it won't happen, but you have to understand there are multitudes of parents who have donated some of their precious biological attributes, their DNA strands, into forming several of the children, but they don't know. They agreed on a higher throne level. And they might not even believe in extraterrestrials! And they may think there's downsides like, "I don't want to pay any more child support!" And they don't understand and they can't understand or they may not be vibrationally compatible. Or people in their household may not be vibrationally compatible. So we are going to focus on the mission. That is why we're here. We're here to focus on the mission. And the relationships will pan out the way that they're supposed to. But if those individuals, those specific individuals, some of them will have those interactions. Like Uncle Ray! Like Uncle Ray! Like Uncle Ray! His two kids are very excited! Very excited! Honey and Red Leaf. Honey and Red Leaf. They're, they've already been in connection with him, but they did not identify themselves. Oooooo! They are now! (Ooooooooo!) He is feeling that love! We might have to change the subject. He might get overwhelmed. (I felt a big surge of love energy!)

Hybrid Children channeled by Ray Heitman 2/15/26
    https://www.youtube.com/watch?v=Uf-f6dkzThQ

Is there a particular protocol for who you will be with when you come to the Earth Mother?

"That is well, yes, and no. There are lots of them, actually. But think of it like this, and this came through in a channeling with Benisha, who is one of our Teachers. Well, that's not the name, but that's the name that they gave because the name that they assume is not really a name. It's more of a frequency. And that's why they can't pronounce it because you can't pronounce frequency other than you could pronounce the word frequency. But it is when we come, we are waiting for the pool to be warm enough, the pool of humanity, so we can go swim in it. And when we come, it'll be mighty chilly. And it will warm up in pockets, some more than others. But that is what we will have to wait for. When it gets to the right temperature, the right vibrational temperature, then we can stick our toe in. And sometimes we might pull it back out. And then we might go in a little bit deeper. And sometimes we will bring toys, and we will ask people to join us. But there will be enclaves. There are special places which are set aside. And those are protected. Those are protected. Yes. And nobody wants to wrestle with a Sasquatch who is protecting the Hybrid Children. You can trust us on that.

"And that will not be the only one (race protecting them). They (Those trying to get to them) will say, "Oh my gosh, I know where they're at. We're going to go get them." And then they'll say, "How did I get here? This is not what I remember. And where are my stuff? Where's my stuff?" And there will be some of that, but that's okay. We're not here to harm people and they aren't here to harm people, but, but there . . . we, we know that they have ways and that in a way is kind of humorous because it will not turn out the way that their plans are intended."

Hybrid Children channeled by Ray Heitman 1/29/26

Where, where do you guys live? Where are you? You somewhere on the Earth somewhere?

"It's a secret planet. It's a secret. It's not a secret! (Okay) The fact, the fact that we live is the only important thing. The fact that we are coming with you is the important thing. And we…not that we cannot answer those questions because we have a biiiig ship. We have lots of biiiig ships! But that…we get our chances. We've been on Earth. We've been in your oceans. We've, we've felt some breeze on our face! But not around you people because it's not time yet. Everything is planned out. This is a mission. And, and we always just do what we're told for the most part because that is what we're allowed to do. And if, if it was up to us, we would tell all of you, you just all raise your vibrations up immediately so we can come tomorrow! But that is not it. We have to do this safely. We have to make sure that you are all aware, and you are all ready, and you are prepared, and you have in ways rid yourself of those beings who are causing the fears which are keeping you down. And you are doing it bit by bit by bit. But it is just a slow unfoldment in your physical linear place. And we are, we are really rejoicing because you have a very funny way which most people do not have -of really thinking while you're talking fast. A lot of people think they, they like sound things out and the ideas come to them but not when they're just machine gunning words out like that! It is nice. It is wonderful. It is a very unique expression. And do not change it. Do not change it. We are just remarking that how remarkable it is. So there you go. It's an attribute, and thank you."

Hybrid Children channeled by Ray Heitman 11/16/25

Do you consider extraterrestrials and humans your parents?

"We have your questions about our parents and it is not really the question which sits well with a lot of humans we would think. Because you ask about our parents. And in truth we believe our parents are just love. Because we were created from love for a loving mission. And the parts really don't matter. They really don't. A little bit here, a little bit there. Apparently, it matters more to the humans than anyone else. So, we do not really consider any one race or any one individual to be a parent. Now, we will put on airs for those humans who are biologically related to us, and not that we are not grateful for their DNA which has gone into assembling us, for making us who we are. But there are many more processes and adjustments and humans have a minority of the biological uh, material which goes into making us.

"But in some ways that makes our artificial wombs part of our parents. And our Teachers and other beings are also considered in that way part of our parents. So we do not accept any lineage or that sort of thing, any genealogical basis or line as valid for us. We just view ourselves as a product of our higher selves, and all of those beings who have taken care of us since before we had our first breath. In a broad way, if you look at your parents, they are the beings who love you and who brought you forth. And we have millions of beings who love us and have brought us forth. Who care for us. Who care about us. Who help us in our various tasks, projects, lessons, the things we learn, and just keeping us company and entertaining us. Anyone who shares with us exhibits that love, exhibits that caring. Which you associate with those parental roles. So that is how we do it. That is how we do it. We just think that love is our parents. And that is probably not the answer that you're looking for, but that is the answer that we have to give. Because it is all matters from the heart, and the heart is all that matters."

Hybrid Children channeled by Ray Heitman 2/26/26
https://youtu.be/P8F1GU_2imo

Have you had an opportunity to interact with autistic children? Um, and if so, in what ways? And what can you teach us?

"We love them. That's all you need to do. You just need to love them, and look out for them. Keep in mind that these, what you determine as autistic children or with other things, are all beings who have chosen to have that express form down to the minutest detail of the atoms within it. They have chosen that because they want what this sperience, experience can give them. They chose that this is the absolute best way to get what they need. It may be to help bring others into the realization of how special and unique all life is, and how humans need to look out for one another. And it is not a coincidence that there are many, many, many autistic children on your planet now. And they are straddling worlds in ways, because their...they all...we won't say all...many of them have that telepathic connection already built in. Now it may not be focused in your world, but they may be communicating with other parts of themselves on a regular basis. And some, as has leaked out into your news or various circles, parents are having telepathic communication with their autistic children. And in other ways there are...um, your technology has allowed some of them to communicate in ways. But, that... like any person on your planet, they all have individual needs... their needs are different. So with the autistic...(sighs)...and this may take some time, but there is the possibility, and the dream state connection is another possibility, but believe they can communicate with you telepathically. Help awaken that. Let them know that you are interested in having them be a bigger part of your life. For they have a different focus...they are more in touch with their nonphysical selves, they just can't bring it out to you so much. Because they do have a narrowed focus. And it is mostly internal, which is an amazing gift because to be active in a physical world based on action and not be able to take a lot of action and being

dependent on many other people just for your existence…well, your survival, you are existence…they want their independence."

Hybrid Children channeled by Ray Heitman 10/5/25
https://www.youtube.com/watch?v=FoxETVnGrlo&t=65s

The Hybrid Children will come to our planet one to five years after Open Contact, which will occur in 2027, and while Open Contact is a certainty, the timing of their arrival depends on how quickly we are ready for them. This will be a gradual implementation, even though it has been going on for over one hundred years. First, we will experience those extraterrestrials who look a lot like us—the Yahyels and Pleiadians, as they are easier to accept. They will be the first extraterrestrial races introduced to the planet on a large scale. I will reveal more about them in a later chapter. They will let us know about the Hybrid Children during the Open Contact events. And after we get used to them and the idea there are many more races coming to Earth, the Hybrid Children will be part of the second wave in my understanding. They will be that vital link to training humans and raising the vibrational frequency of the planet so even more beings with even higher vibrational frequencies can safely interact with us. They will do so just by being their adorable, infectious, loving selves. But we must create the vibrational frequency that will allow them to safely come here first by establishing a "middle ground" for safe contact, meaning our own vibrations must be able to handle their energy.

"There are several 'phases' of the Hybrid Children coming down. In total, for the overall first phase, there will be 333 Hybrid Children that will come to Earth in that first phase. Most of the first group of the 333 will be what you would call teenagers. They will get younger as the teenagers pave the way for the younger ones to come later, who will need more training and more time to acclimate

to your society. " Bashar session titled "Dear Mom and Dad" 2016
https://www.facebook.com/share/p/18BsyD4vBh/

"There are Hybrid Children that are on your planet. Some of them do know they are hybrids, and yes, some of them have been adopted by human companions, parents in that way. So, this has happened. Yeah. They, Hybrid Children, have many different pathways of integration into your society. Some Hybrid Children play more of a background role at this time. Simply observing. Sometimes projecting into your reality. Exploring the neighborhoods, exploring the cities, exploring the different communities. And then when they have received the experiences they require for their lesson learning, they withdraw themselves. For other Hybrid Children, they have chosen to play a much more "boots on the ground" role, if you will, and some of them have a life with situations where they ultimately become adopted by human parents. This occurs as well, and this has happened. And is currently happening."

Ryokah channeled by Tyler Ellison. Posted on his Facebook page 4/4/25

Although it is a well-kept secret outside of those who follow major channelers, some Hybrid Children have been living on Earth for decades. Most have been in rather secluded environments or smaller communities, with many brought to families via adoption agencies. When the first wave of Hybrid Children comes in after Open Contact, they will be gathered in secure enclaves in carefully chosen locations and will have little contact with humans who are not involved with them. This will help them acclimate to the Earth's gravity and seasons and further prepare them for their new life "planet-side." They will be carefully watched, as well as the reactions of the local and worldwide populace, to help gauge when the time for more adventurous interactions will be safe before venturing among us in limited and then more expansive ways. It is important to keep our focus on the love they are bringing, and to allow that feeling to grow in our hearts, and to express it in our thoughts and actions, so we can help prepare ourselves and our communities to accept them.

And now for the rest of the Open Contact love story! It is so exciting for me! As Open Contact Event is a love story of heart connections encompassing the whole planet, as it involves all life upon it and our connections to loving beings from the skies. It is best viewed from the perspective of the heart. The unselfish things we do for those we love are analogous to what the coming extraterrestrials wish to do for us. They wish to help us grow and lead more loving lives, free of fear and the struggle to stay alive. Restoring the natural balance and harmony to our planet is part of that. After Open Contact, the extraterrestrials will bring us technological wonders like free energy and healing medbeds, as well as show us new ways to improve our food quality and quantity and introduce us to the great wide world which exists outside our own. They have been waiting a long, long time to bestow those gifts upon us, but if they came too soon, they would disrupt our planet and cause chaos. They have done so before with other civilizations and learned their lesson, and now follow strict protocols and conduct a lot of testing and monitoring to make sure the actions taken do not have significant adverse effects.

There will always be skeptics and those who are suspicious, as we have been taught to fear lots of things by our parents, communities, and religions. Things like strangers, large animals, storms, a wrathful and vengeful God, and countless other things based on instilling fear and obedience. Those beliefs that may have been thought to be useful at some point are no longer valid. We are moving into a reality where those beliefs will be exposed as baseless and will eventually fade into history. This love story is a story of togetherness, openness, and unity where communities, societies, and an entire planet come together to repair the damage of the disaster we have made of our planet and to learn to value, honor, and protect all diverse life on it. A love story of being truly heart-focused and heart-centered, where we respond with love first, like our extraterrestrial friends do. They will treat us as equals because they understand that when one succeeds, we all succeed. That is what a unified consciousness is all about—the joyful open sharing of love in all its forms. That is the reality we are building; we have already started, and there is no turning back. Open Contact will happen and is part of that change, but it is not the impetus for it. We have to initiate the change, and then those loving beings will help us move it forward to the stars. The old adage that *love wins* is true, but sometimes it takes 2,000 or so years in our time, reckoning for that to be realized. The joy of discovering ourselves and building a New Earth where all consciousness can thrive and a new species of humanity can evolve—homo galacticus. And each of us chose to incarnate here and now to be a part of it.

The missions of Open Contact have been carefully and meticulously planned by experts and will be carried out by beings who are trained and experienced, like the Hybrid Children. We can trust them, and we will trust them, but that trust requires acceptance and an integration which must proceed in measured steps. The more we lead with our hearts, the faster it will settle in. In the future, you will encounter the term "First Contact specialist," which is a primary designation for beings who assist other planets and cultures in becoming more cohesive, love-oriented societies, and who are trained to approach and build awareness of star beings so that those changes take hold gracefully. I first heard that term from Bashar, a Sassani being who is a First Contact specialist channeled by Darryl Anka. More on that race and their role later.

The Hybrid Children and extraterrestrials who will be known to us openly in 2027 are the proverbial "Welcome Wagon" from our galactic neighbors, and they are giving us the opportunity to get to know them before they come to interact with and live amongst humans freely on our planet. That process will flow in stages, starting by showing us we are not the only intelligence in our universe and then providing more information and secrets about them and our planet's history, bit by bit. Mysteries like the Egyptian pyramids, Atlantis, Lemuria, the true history of Earth, the creation of our solar system, and much, much more. Once enough of us come to a realization that they are real and desire more, we will be ready to learn more and accept their help. The coming disclosures by our governments and by other more reliable sources will shed more light on our extraterrestrial friends.

Ancient knowledge of extraterrestrials has been passed down from generation to generation and kept alive by indigenous cultures in stories that have been threaded into our current times over countless centuries. We have always had clues, and throughout history, there have always been those who gave us these truths. Many of them were persecuted by those in power for disclosing that knowledge, but the knowledge has persisted. There have been repeated sightings of spaceships for many decades, and millions of people know the story of the Roswell incident; soon, they will know the whole truth behind it. Other clues of extraterrestrial involvement and sightings are emerging daily. The proliferation of channelers around the globe is part of the Open Contact scenario, for each channeler not only brings forth information from nonhuman entities, but each such interaction also allows more high-vibrational energy into our collective energetic environment, further raising the collective vibrational frequency of our planet. Those interactions and connections literally anchor a connective thread from galactic beings and higher realms into our chosen reality of Earth. As more people awaken, seek answers to mysteries, and heed the impulse to learn more, those energies will continue to take hold and lift us and our planet higher, which in turn will help awaken even more people. That cycle of love and unity will grow and ripple out until it eventually encircles the entire planet.

Other stories foretelling this point in our future have been around for centuries. Stories of the Awakening, Ascension, and visitors from the skies and the wonders they will bring have existed since before written languages came into being. Stories of space "gods" interacting with humans and bringing them precious gifts of knowledge will come true in tangible ways in our near future, and Open Contact is the significant turning point in humanity's evolution. Only these are not gods. They are our equals, coming with more experience to share the love and gifts they have to offer. And that is where the Hybrid Children come in. They are the bridge to our future. They will pave the way by anchoring even more unconditional love and sharing into our planet, and they are designed and created to fit in this time in our history in just the right place—our hearts.

"The Hybrid Children bring with them energy and codes that connect and attune with Mother Earth's grids and thus their energies flow freely with Mother Earth's energies helping to raise the vibrational frequencies of humankind, which bring about much healing of old paradigms, old thought processes, old energies that no longer serve humankind that can hold back peoples from a society of compassion and opening of the heart. Their energies will meld and blend with humankind, and many, many who are attuned already to this energy will blend their energy as their energy will blend in as well, aligning with the higher vibrational frequencies. The specifics of the different types of Hybrid Children are as numerous as each individual child for there are, there are many with many purposes to contribute to the overall ascension process occurring at this time. For we are all, many of us, ascending. You (Ray) have connections with the Hybrid Children in a unique way in that you are one of the bridging individuals acting in a role of bridging energies. Those that come in contact with you will feel a vibrational lift."

Heidi Slater, Divine Love Collective 11/30/25
   https://youtu.be/mpTbwgjagDk

But first, we have to prove to the extraterrestrials that we are ready and able to accept their presence by initiating changes in our societies to show that we are moving towards a more peaceful, loving planet. We need leaders who look out for all life on the planet and the planet itself, rather than those who abuse their power and exploit other people and resources for the few. Those changes are happening, and many more are coming in the next two years to set the stage for even greater changes and for Open Contact to occur. That too is part of the grander mission to help humanity ascend to new heights, but the stage has to be cleared of the "bad actors" before the more qualified, heart-based performers can begin to lead the next act of our play. It will happen, and there are many surprises coming. It is our time.

"Now, there are other races besides ours which are helping to coordinate and design and entertain protocols and studies and methods of learning for the Hybrid Children. And there are a great many ways, and some of those will be coming to your planet, to help enrich the educational opportunities for many of your youngsters, and those who wish to learn who may be of an adult stature, we will say. Now, we hope that this little bit of information has been helpful to you. And we enjoy viewing and absorbing and introspecting all of the related events around the context scenarios which are forthcoming, and the Hybrid Children are a major part of that, as after the initial wave of excitement circles your Earth many, many times from the contact which is forthcoming. Once it recedes a little, then the Hybrid Children will be welcomed in greater numbers, and we look forward to that. It brings great joy to us, and if you knew, it would bring great joy to you as well. Celebrate those future moments which are coming, and trust us, you cannot celebrate enough."

Future Pleiadians channeled by Ray Heitman 5/28/25
   https://www.youtube.com/watch?v=C0eJ2g8LQv4&t=4s

The role of the Hybrid Children after Open Contact is an easy one—they will be themselves! By doing so, they will impact humanity and the Earth physically and psychologically. The physical impacts are all a result of their higher vibration frequency and nutrition education. They will raise the vibration of anyone they encounter, which will help us feel more love, be more loving, and allow us to release some energies trapped in our bodily cells. And the Hybrid Children will teach us how to not only imbue our food and drink with beneficial energy, but help introduce us to better methods of nutrition, food preparation, and storage, literally making us healthier in mind and body. And our higher vibration will benefit other humans when we encounter them, as it will raise their vibration, just as when all energies connect and affect each other. Like when happy people lift others up! It is the best joyous energy epidemic ever—contagious heart energy and love! And that higher vibrational life will open up insights and spiritual growth opportunities for individuals and groups as well, as the higher we vibrate, the more doors of opportunity and the more free-flowing our lives become. As the Hybrid Children told me, "It is opening minds and opening hearts," and is the biggest transformation of consciousness our planet has ever seen. The higher vibrations will affect all consciousness on the planet, which is known outside of Earth as the Earth Collective.

"You take other people with you like they are hanging on to your capes, and you are rising up higher and higher, and all these other people are saying, 'Wow, this is cool. Thanks for showing me this new pathway, this growth and expansion of my own self. Wow, just by being around you have lifted me up.' And that is what we try to do too. We will. We will, because our vibration is higher than yours. Not that that is a bad thing. It is just a factoid."

Hybrid Children channeled by Ray Heitman 7/21/25

https://youtu.be/42-8syb-hmE

The psychological impacts on our societies will be many-layered. It will come from the Hybrid Children, giving people something positive and exciting to talk about and giving them hope for the future. That excitement and optimism will help many lose their fears and be more confident and willing to accept the changes to come. We will feel things are improving and will continue to improve, lifting the vibrations of millions and millions, all of which makes for a glorious wave of love energy spreading a blanket of good cheer all over the planet. Here are a few quotes to help drive home their impact…

"We are coming to Earth to play and to reawaken that inner child in all of your humans, at least the ones who had a lot of fun and who felt safe and free to explore. That is what we are doing, coming to your Earth. That is our role on Earth. To be an example, to show humans how to love unconditionally and how to love all unconditionally, and how to play, and to give them the example of singing and dancing and sharing all the time. To find ways to incorporate that into their being because it lifts them up so much. It raises their vibration. It opens up paths of exploration and growth for them. It greatly expands their opportunities for further growth and advancement in soul-fulfilling ways."

Hybrid Children channeled by Ray Heitman 1/6/26
   https://youtu.be/goIS1nMzRC4

"It is not so much the categories of the specific job duties or whatever we may have, that those are roles for other beings, and not that we won't participate in them, because we have a lot of knowledge and we have learned how to integrate them by the time we get there anyway. But our main role is to be ourselves and to let you know that the coming beings, which are on the way, on the way, on the way, are safe and you can trust them! And you can trust us! And we will help to point out some of the areas in which you can improve, just so people think about them, not so much to introduce them to the technologies

and processes which will help them, but to get them to think about those ideas, so when they are presented, they will be accepted in a more ready fashion. We will say so that it will slide into your societies, and not so much your power structures, which you have created or which have been created, but it is opening minds and opening hearts. It is building awareness of what could be. That is our role."

Hybrid Children channeled by Ray Heitman 1/6/26
https://youtu.be/golS1nMzRC4

"It (this book) will be a turning point itself in the lives of many people because it will bring that awareness. It will shake them up and say, 'Hey, looks like we got love on the way.' And that is a grand, glorious thing. For many, humans haven't had hope, really significant hope, for quite some time, and we will bring that. And it's more of a knowing than it is a hope. We will bring that knowing that things are getting better, that there is much to look forward to. So it is more of a psychological role, while it does have its physical attributes, because raising the vibration is definitely a physical attribute, but it will help people to feel better. That is a lovely, lovely thing, to have them feel more love in their lives, for them to whistle and be happy and to sing, and that will affect everyone around them, as you know."

Hybrid Children channeled by Ray Heitman 1/6/26
https://youtu.be/golS1nMzRC4

This new wave of love and positive expectations will help us accept and integrate the changes our world needs to grow and become a unified whole. Let's examine some of those from the perspective of the Hybrid Children. Keep your heart and mind open, as some of these changes may seem a bit radical, but will be accepted in the New Earth we are creating. To put it bluntly, accepted beliefs and societal norms, life experiences, and patterned behaviors of "it is how life is" or should be, are outdated and do not fit the new paradigm and reality to come. These changes will be a shock to many, but if you think about them, they all make sense. I love each and every one of them and look forward to doing my part to implement them.

After Open Contact, part of our unification process will be to eliminate country boundaries. The Hybrid Children are certainly in favor of this, as you can see in this quote.

"Geography is...not a favorite. We...ugh...humans have arbitrary lines that they fight over. It, it, ahhh. We don't...we don't...we...ahhh...we just view it as a whole. And we understand groupings and communities, but the larger structures which you conform to are somewhat bothersome to us for they do not have a real reason, and they are created out of lack and fears and controlling efforts and distrust. And wuh...there's no need for those types of boundaries! Especially when they're only on paper and views on digital objects. But even if there are boundaries of rivers or mountains, then let's treat them all as one and just say it is a magnificent part of Gaia, and then it belongs to Gaia, and she will take care of it, and we can go about seeking ways of betterment."

Hybrid Children channeled by Ray Heitman 5/22/25
https://www.youtube.com/watch?v=qzrapAYNogk

"Today we are looking at all of the different ways we can stop humans from using trees for various products. Yeah. We are exploring...not even from your pencils and your toilet paper and your building supplies—all of them will have to be changed because we need to protect the trees. We need to make more trees. We need to keep the trees happy and healthy and reproducing. And, have them contribute more energy by having more of them to the rescue of your planet. The reinstatement of the natural balances and energies and gridlines. And other things too on your planet. And that will help bring the elementals, and lots of other positive love energies into more of a contact with humans."

"And we need to do away with your grass lawns. Absolutely! That is one of the things which will change. I hope they get legislated out of existence because they do nothing but poison your Earth, waste your human's time, and create lots and lots of chemicals which are spread all over the land, in the stream, in the rivers, and in the oceans. And they have such a horrible effect on all of the critters and Mother Nature overall because they ruin the energies! Those energies of even all of the stuff you plant cannot give off their greatest, truest vibration, and emanations because they are muted and they are treated with such . . . it is like the . . . it is even worse than the GMO stuff because they are cultivated to do certain things and not to allow other things to do their thing. And that is just a restriction which is unimaginable for conscious beings."

Hybrid Children channeled by Ray Heitman 10/13/25
https://youtu.be/XVx2WqJ47CY

Chapter Six

A Teacher's Perspective

This chapter came about after the Hybrid Children told me I would channel one of their Teachers to "round out" the book's information. Luckily for all of us, I take direction well. I was overly excited at the prospect! Not only because I had not channeled one of their Teachers before, but I get excited at channeling any new entity, as I know it will help me prepare for my own personal Open Contact experience and to be able to mingle with many different extraterrestrial races in the future. Then, when I received a message from the Future Pleiadians on 1/22/26 that today was the day to bring in one of the Yahyel Teachers, I was elated to the point of jumping for joy. It was a huge deal for me. I quickly made arrangements for a member of High Vibe Channeling, Luis Don Al Suarez, to join us. I provided Luis with the questions I had for the Teacher, and he added quite a few of his own, which greatly added to the information they provided. Shortly before the session started, I received the name Baneesha at a stoplight while returning from an errand and was told it was the name of the Teacher who would join us for the session. I am guessing at the spelling. In this session, they provided comprehensive details about the Hybrid Children and the roles of the Teachers and Watchers, but like any helicopter parent, they were focused on the Hybrid Children more than interacting with me the whole time.

They discussed a wide variety of topics, such as their missions and how, as a cohesive group, they teach the Hybrid Children. They also touched on the role the Watchers fulfill in educating them, how the Hybrid Children's needs are determined and addressed, how they control their curriculum, and quite a bit of information related to the Hybrid Children already or formerly living on Earth and the role of those no longer on Earth after Open Contact. They also touched on the process of the integration of Hybrid Children into our societies, how they experience humans, and how Open Contact and humanity benefit extraterrestrials. All information was relayed by a loving expert whose life's passion is nurturing and providing for those who are loving bridges to our future. The vast majority of this information is not available elsewhere, and I am in awe at the detail and breadth of the information provided. I was also told Baneesha had no interest in coming to Earth and was very satisfied to spend all of his/her time with the Hybrid Children. The entire transcript of that session is below, including time stamps. Please understand Baneesha is not used to using any language, let alone English, so at times the wrong word is chosen, and then the correct wording will follow. You can find the full video on the High Vibe Channeling YouTube channel session titled "Yahyel Teacher Baneesha Explains the Teacher's Roles."

2:03 into the video

Baneesha: And this is a new experience for us in this way. We come to you in brotherhood, and we bring to you our love and our heart. For we are wrapped up in the same event, the same preparations, so to speak, just in different levels, in different guises. And while our name is not pronounced in human form, you may call us that "Beneesha" and we shall associate with it.

Luis: Thank you, Beneesha.

Beneesha: And we are indeed one of the Teachers. And there are many of us. And we are able to ascertain, in your terms, the questions of the individual who is helping in the mission by completing his book. And this suggestion, like many others, were given to the Hybrid Children, for they are indeed more focused on play and how they can use what is before them in humorous ways than our conveying the information which may be of service to you and yours. We have come

118

today to impress upon you not only the importance of your missions but the importance of the overall mission. For although it has all been determined and exists in other ways than your linear forms, that is an energetic reality which has yet to unfold in what you consider timelines which are merely variations of events, paths leading up to the same summit on your mountains. In ways the categories of Teachers are not as rigid as what you would have assumed. We have no specific subjects which one (Teacher) will cover, for we all are interconnected in those ways. And while we have our specialties and we have our own personal desires and favorites, those are based on a frequency match more than they are a desire which comes forth from the environment like it does with humans. And all of us are capable to bring forth the particular lessons which are needed for we are all drawing from the same field of information in your terms, the same wellspring of knowledge. And while we may come about it in different ways, that mainly depends upon the audience to which we are coming to.

5:35 into the video

Beneesha: For different Hybrid Children have different (pause), we do not wish to say more appropriate, but ways of integration which fit better with their natural tendencies. And the Watchers themselves are merely special guests in the lesson curriculum. For instance, if we are speaking of, or teaching of, a particular planetary system or society, and we have one of those beings available, they will come in and help to provide more detailed information via frequencies more often than what you would consider language or communication in that way. For most carry pictures, visuals of events in their individual lives, and others which are referenced and can be provided to the lovely children. We call them children, for they are the only children which we have on our ships. And that (Watcher visuals) will help in filling in the nuances and helping them get a fuller comprehension of the lessons themselves. And all of those beings are not as playful as what the children would like, but that is to be expected.

7:17 into the video

Beneesha: And while they may be joyful in spirit, for instance, the Mantis beings just are not engaging in that way of play. As your Tall Whites, which come through this channel, are not engaged in play in that way. Amongst their own kind, they can be quite frivolous, for there are ways of expression which are more readily accepted, we will say. As far as the curriculum, it is chosen by many. And it depends on the mission and the progress that humans are making. For indeed, there are fine-tunings and levels, such as learning your languages and adaptations, for instance, your melanin has to be adjusted for certain individuals when they prove to be a better fit or a more adequate subject for engaging a particular geographic area on your planet. Have we covered the main subjects which the channeler wishes to achieve in this interaction?

8:44 into the video

Luis: The main subjects you have, but I'd like to see if we can go a little bit deeper.

Baneesha: Please do so. We are here at your service.

Luis: So rather than focus on the various different kinds of Teachers, I'd like to ask how are they being prepared emotionally, vibrationally? How are they being trained in terms of social skills? What is it that is being emphasized in the current training for the children?

Baneesha: We, we ask for clarification and only one question at a time, please. Are you addressing the Teachers' needs or the children's needs?

Luis: I am addressing what the children need and are receiving.

Baneesha: How do you learn what your children need?

Luis: Resonance, energy to me, you know, for me.

Baneesha: You know what they need for survival. You hope that you need or you know what they need for their growth, and you do the best you can with the knowledge and the resources you have at hand. This is no different. Only we have all of the resources and knowledge, not even at hand, but innate within us. And those, too, are changed as the needs of the children change. So there need be no set protocol. It is merely a flowing. And as they express their own interests, that is taken into consideration, and the future educational needs are adjusted. For some do indeed have certain aptitude for other things. Some prefer to specialize in human contact, some in animal contact, or environmental needs. Some in rejoicing with the spirit realms. Some in extraterrestrial, in your terms, contact and teaching them about humans. There are many, many roles, and each child picks what they prefer. We do not hamper them in any way or lead them into other ways, for it all flows naturally. And should there be what you would consider a "gap" in the mission protocol, or an individual to fill a specific slot, they are merely created to fill that in. And that, in that way, there is no hampering of the adjustments or the desires or the educational fun lessons that the children wish to undertake. We merely work around their particular focuses to make sure that all is accomplished.

12:00 into the video

Luis: We will be moving to cohabitation. So the children will be habitating with families.

Baneesha: It will be some time, except for those who are already on your planet.

Luis: Oh, okay. I wanted to talk about the ones that are already on the planet a little bit. If you could shed any information about that.

12:26 into the video

Baneesha: They are test subjects, you may say. They are more advanced of the Hybrid Children, and they have been schooled in different ways. And while they are in touch with the Hybrid Children on the ships, (pause) they do not relay all of their information for the children are not ready for that in their ways. The children on your planet have difficulties, for the humans are not like them. And that is not the difficulty. It is the fact that the humans do not believe, and they do not perform, they have behaviors which are not like them. Withholding something from someone or something in need is abhorrent and would never be done by a Hybrid Child. They tend to recall, recoil when they experience a being who is suffering and no one reaches out to help. They have many quiet times in this and they must be consoled by other entities which are nearby and always in touch. But they do enjoy the loving expressions, like the pets. But some of them are in homes, which although the lessons are valuable, is a rather tough challenge for those particular children. And they have to be adjusted in ways. And some of them choose to leave early as opposed to continuing their mission. So they are, they will succumb to circumstances, we will say. With our blessing, for it is indeed each of those heroes' choices.

14:46 into the video

Baneesha: And ones which have come into contact with the cruelty of others do not embrace that energy. And it is difficult enough for them to have a reduced role and not to fulfill their innate desires and objectives of playing and sharing and loving without having them to purposely interact with beings who exhibit what you have called low-vibrational behaviors. And they can handle those to a limited degree, but we do not wish to scar them in that way. And after they do leave the physical plane, they become great Teachers themselves in the spirit realm. For there are indeed Hybrid Children who have gone over to spirit, which act as Teachers and guides. And they will continue to do so until they choose otherwise and pursue their own soulful destinations. They are indeed glorified and revered by all who know them, just as your Hybrid Children will be when they come planet-side.

Luis: So these are essentially souls of great service, and they are on a mission that serves, not just humanity, but the consciousness of all the beings that exist in this universe.

Baneesha: They are guides. You may consider them probes that you send out so they can take samples of various parts of planetary surfaces or asteroids, as it may be. They take readings. They relay back information, and that information becomes integrated into the other plans. And some of them thrive better than others. Most of that is an environmental capacity to accept those changes and to minimize the effect of some of the negative aspects, but in some cases, where there is, we do not like to use the term abuse, but that is appropriate. And it may not be and is not the families who have taken it upon themselves to integrate those beings into their units, but those outside of the family units who interact with them are not always of like mind and do not always reach heart first for those children when they interact with them. Unfortunately, you are well accustomed to those behaviors, amongst others, and know of them.

18:13 into the video

Luis: Yes, indeed. It's difficult for sure, even for a human that has an open heart. I see that there will still be children that will be here at the time in which we start actually making Open Contact with these children. In other words, they are here now, and they will be here then. How will their roles grow as they are here?

18:47 into the video

Baneesha: They will be freed of their bonds of not, or of pretending who they are not. Such as you, when you encounter a large group and all of a sudden you find out there is someone from your hometown who speaks your language, who will understand the nuances of what you are trying to convey. And you instantly form a bond with them. And you share the commonalities, and there are smiles radiating abundantly. It will be a homecoming of sorts. And for specific parental units or accompaniments, they may join those particular children as they are included in the enclaves. There may be a period of adjustment. And it all depends on the mission parameters, which are foremost and topnotch, topmost, and those must be the focus—always. For that is what we are all striving towards. And even if that is not expressed, that is the desired goal of the millions of beings who are not humans who are involved in these processes of transformation and leading and educating humans into better use of their resources, human and planet-wise. Not to mention the energies of the aetheric, aethereal rain, realms. And those beings who they will be in connection with. There will not need to be a "reeducation" in those ways, but there may be some limited segregation from the main population of the children to come. Because those children are kept in, in seclusion in some ways, and buffered from the actions of humanity. And while they may know of them, they know of them in an indirect way when we can help it. They do not come into contact with those frequencies themselves. And they will be awakened to some of the possibilities when they do.

21:31 into the video

Luis: Yeah, that addresses something that was in my mind. That the adjustments to their light bodies and their energetic fields will have to be massive as they mingle more and more with humanity.

Baneesha: It will not be difficult, for they will be gradually eased in, and likewise humanity will be eased into them. It will be a slow process. This will not be a scattering. This will be a slow melding. And only those environments which are helpful, which aid in the mission, will be allowed to experience them in a more open climate, we will say.

Luis: What would you like to disseminate to the people here on the planet that have an openness to Hybrid Children, as what can I say, an instruction set on how they should be preparing the ground around themselves for this major event?

22:56 into the video

Baneesha: They need to emulate the Hybrid Children when at all possible. Some of the more drastic consequences of lifting a hand to help others have been removed in your societies. Those who exhibit the vulnerability of aiding strangers do not have to worry, in ways, about violence coming back to them. Now, those who have called that as part of their plan or as part of their beliefs will still experience that as part of the schoolroom Earth they have chosen. But in general, those good deeds will be rewarded and not punished, as that contrasting phrase goes in your vocabulary. So if they do reach out and they make it a point to lead heart first, see it is not what the individuals do so much to help the Hybrid Children. It is what the individuals do to lift up those around them and those who they encounter to help spread that vibrational lift, to create an overall environment where they may come in. You might say the pool is too cold for the children to swim, and each interaction with humans helps warm it up a bit. And as those spread out, then the pool will soon become warm enough for all to swim together.

24:46 into the video

Luis: What message can we spread to those with whom we have the ability to be in any kind of contact?

Baneesha: We urge...

Luis: Yeah, go ahead.

Baneesha: We urge you not to spread or think about any message, but merely to show them by your example. That is the best way in this particular time to awaken the many, for the words are still tainted. The actions are not. And after they encounter a couple of loving actions, they will think about doing so themselves or discuss those events with others. And, innately, it will pass between those individuals telepathically that the world is changing. Things are getting better.

Luis: Indeed, there's evidence that I see on a daily basis. Even though the big things don't appear to, but that's just the nature of change, basically. Going back to the children that are here already, and as you said, some will be here for the long run, and some will not. Uh, and that's part of the plan. A number of different reasons for that, of course. But those that are, as they continue to, you know, in a linear time sense age, they will be able to get into some positions of what we're going to call Earthly power. What do you guys see there?

Baneesha: They do not wish to have that type of notoriety. They may be entrepreneurs in the arts, and some of those children are now in your linear terms in their 20s. They will be brought forth to help communicate to humans. Some in public forums to help educate them on the children to come, and to help acclimate them and answer some of their questions. Especially where they are known in those communities, in those groups. And if you think about it, that is a natural way to progress the acceptance of the overall mission of leading to having extraterrestrials live amongst you and not bat an eye.

Luis: Beautiful. Are the children aware of the multiple timelines that are available?

Baneesha: They are aware of what they need to be aware. They know of them, but if it is not relevant, it never enters their thoughts. If you are watching a program or a movie which you are intensely involved in, you do not care what are any of the other channels or options which are available. That is more of the same in an analogy for you.

Luis: It's a beautiful analogy. Yeah, indeed. And how are the galactic lineages that bring us to this place continuing their efforts to integrate?

Baneesha: Those terms is not valid. The lineages of which you speak are frequently of longer terms than your centuries by far. And all different races do not have the same biology and do not provide offspring in your ways of reckoning, the way, or in any way which you would conceive of. They may merely send out offshoots of them (themselves) and have those off, offshoots cross different barriers in

126

which they manifest in those particular realms in different ways. And that is the best example that we can give you.

Luis: Yeah.

Baneesha: For you are indeed a type of energy which outside of this particular realm has a completely different form. If you consider that a form.

Luis: Sure. How do the children see us? The awakened adults.

Baneesha: They do not see you in the way which you mean. They experience you with a myriad of senses, many of which you do not have incorporated in your chosen biology, your form. They experience you on a variety of levels, even within that, for they are able to detect your energetic essences prior to manifestations. They will have foreknowledge of events to come, for they can see laterally the possibilities and the probabilities of those future unfoldments which humans have chosen to keep from their knowing.

Luis: There's much that we can learn from that.

Baneesha: That is an understatement. (Yeah.) We thank you for bringing it up.

Luis: I'm in awe for sure. And to be here is an honor.

Baneesha: And we must, well, we "must" is the wrong word, but we sense it is a valuable bit of information that the particular, the children which are coming are going to easily be more accepted by the feminine forms on your planet. For the patriarchy and those who have chosen to limit their emotional expressions will find it hard at first to break their identities which they are familiar with. In time those hearts will melt. Those patterns of behavior will erode, and they, too, will embrace the children with loving open arms. But they will pretend in their ways and stick to their roles they have chosen. Their macho sensibilities and actions, and the boundaries they have set for those. But, you are losing those. Thankfully so. But that is one aspect of coming in which will take some time before full acceptance will be allowed. Your younger generations shall not have that issue. They are more accepting, except in those homes where those overriding masculine overtones are predominant.

33:16 into the video

Luis: It has been said that 2050 or thereabouts is a major place where a lot of these things begin to merge and become more prevalent on the planet. But I tend to think personally that we're looking at an entirely, entirely, entirely different realm here around the proximity of the end of this century.

Baneesha: It has yet to be determined.

Luis: So you're saying it could even take longer.

Baneesha: We are saying it is dependent on many factors. Many of which are beyond your understanding. Acceptance and a loving heart will bring them in faster. Resistance, like everything in your physical realm, will make things more challenging, difficult, barrier-filled. If you go with that loving flow.

Luis: It will flow.

Baneesha: It will flow.

Luis: Yeah, I got that. Flow.

Baneesha: You will always experience rapids on your trip downstream, but some of them are easier to avoid or to navigate than others. It depends on who is steering the boat and the type of boat you choose.

Luis: It seems like we are getting a lot of benefit out of these interactions that we've been having with all of you; the children, the Teachers, and other architects of the program. Question is, how much are you guys gaining through these interactions?

Baneesha: That is (pause) an understatement, for you do not realize the impact of being Teachers yourselves to all of these other races. To watch you and your kind bloom in ways from the darkness, the abyss which you have submerged yourself in, and to come up to the surface smiling and say, "See what we have learned. Let us show you." It is not so much for *us*, for we know what the futures are for you. It is for the joy which we feel in providing our part of our mission. And if it is engaging with humans, then we shall with full open hearts and desires. It will be for those who have those missions their greatest desires. For us, we, me in particular, it is the children. They are our only focus. They are more important than our individual sustenance or fulfillment, for they are one and the same in ways which is hard for humans to comprehend. They are the beat of our heart.

Luis: Yeah, it's all about the heart. I think the unity of hearts. I guess.

37:11 into the video

Baneesha: We are approaching the end of this interaction. And we thank you for aiding this one (Ray) in obtaining the information he desired, which shall be incorporated and which shall aid in the fulfillment of those who encounter the book.

Luis: Yes, very important book.

Baneesha: And we bless you as you have blessed us with your time and your energy. It is greatly appreciated and received. And we hope, and you will, receive benefit in kind. (End of Session)

The Yahyel Teacher Baneesha channeled by Ray Heitman 1/22/26
https://www.youtube.com/watch?v=aJWAlbFh_CU&t=2s

What an amazing resource Baneesha is! I was very impressed with the intense love I felt for the love and dedication Baneesha had for the Hybrid Children, and I felt it strongly. It was endearing and unwavering, like the most protective animal kingdom parents. To me the resonance of their devotion meant those precious children's lives were of the utmost value, possibly worth more than their own in a human way of thinking, and if that behavior and focus is indicative of all of the Yahyel Teachers what a great treasure they must be to take care of a treasure like the Hybrid Children. I am fortunate to feel the love of this connection and information, and the fact they consider my channeling of them part of the Open Contact scenario.

To take time away from overseeing of various aspects of the Hybrid Children along with other Open Contact responsibilities speaks of its importance, and their energy is also behind this book, as are many other interested extraterrestrial races and groupings, because it is part of the Open Contact event. It helps to bring awareness of not only the event, but to awaken the relationships we are destined to have. We will learn about as many space races as we desire, as no information will be held back. All extraterrestrials involved in Open Contact will lovingly share what they know to the best of their ability, but also aid in teaching you how to ask better questions so you know what to ask. Each contact will initially be geared to aid in specific and general comprehension and energetic tolerances related to current and future encounters and energies, and to test readiness for them. Our success and futures are important enough to the participants in Open Contact and they are delighted we humans are progressing in the linear unfoldment of the success and quality of life and evolution of our planet and everything on it, and to partner with us helping other galaxies

For me personally the details of the design, creation, and orchestration of Open Contact just from the little inside peek I receive from sessions like this one from Baneesha leaves me in amazed awe. But Baneesha is but one of the millions of extraterrestrials in humanities futures. A future where our lives flow with a synchronicity humans will dream into being, with the help of various races, energies, and various alliances. There is much to learn not only about the Yahyel and their role with the Hybrid Children, but about our many galactic friends and family and all the details about them and what they do our minds can hold. The roles of extraterrestrials in our futures and those of our children's descendants and the explorations we share with them on Earth and beyond are part of the dream of a peaceful world where all consciousness is valued, like Baneesha values the Hybrid Children.

Chapter Seven

How Can We Help the Hybrid Children?

Someone asked the Hybrid Children, "How can we help you?" in a High Vibe Channeling session, and they responded immediately: "Play more! Play more! Play more! Play more!" While that is an energetic and truthful answer, this multilayered question has multilayered answers. The answer to this question is to be more like the Hybrid Children themselves and to connect with them. The first part of that answer is to be your authentic self, the self you desire you and everyone else to be. The one with the highest vibrational frequency. The one who follows their highest excitement to the best of their ability, is free from worry and thoughts that do not lift them up, and who plays and enjoys life regardless of circumstances by maintaining their mind and bodily form in its best possible condition, and who looks out for others in a heartfelt, compassionate way. It all comes down to the expression of our vibrational frequency—the quantity and quality of love we can accept, hold, and give. We incarnated now to be a part of the transformation of humanity and our Earth. We chose this! And love makes all the difference.

"You guys are continuing to build on your vibration. We're getting good reports, and it is coming. Open Contact is coming! Open Contact is coming! You still have lots of work to do. You have work to do. You have to, you have to kick some of that negativity to the curb and, and, and restore a bunch of hope and love and, and

community...sense of community to each other and, and across the world. And once you feel, if you feel that you are in a...um, that everyone else is your brethren, then you will find that you will have visitors from the skies. Because you have to get there before we can get here. So hurry up, hurry up, hurry up, because we want to play with you in person, and we wish to create, and we wish to see all the joys on the human's faces when they understand what they are going to have. Oh my gosh, it is so exciting!"

Hybrid Children channeled by Ray Heitman 7/20/25
https://youtu.be/PfL32pjY-bo

"We want you to be overjoyed and happy, and we wish to bring you up. And we wish to help keep you there with your loving thoughts and energies which you all have inside you, which sometimes you do not use enough. That love stuff is just so vitallll! And sometimes you hold it in. And we would rather share, share, share! And make sure that everyone is aware of how special they are and how well needed, how, how, how vital they are to us and to the overall energies and realms in which we participate and belong to."

Hybrid Children channeled by Ray Heitman 6/1/25
https://www.youtube.com/watch?v=2tOkl6UUrpg&t=17s

"And one of the reasons why we enjoy and engage with so many different types of individuals and why we are so excited about meeting with humans, because we can share ourselves with them! We can share so...we have so much to share and so much love to give. And so many things that we would like to experience with you to make it even more special for all involved. Those are kind of our dreams. And we think, and we build up expectations, happy expectations, energetic expectations, of interactions with humans. And as you may have guessed, then...that not only...draws those events closer to us."

Hybrid Children channeled by Ray Heitman 6/7/25

"But you have to get there first. You have to get there. Even if you buy a ticket, you have to get to the event. That is what you are doing. You are buying tickets with each positive impact that you make, every person on your planet. And you are going to fill the skies with positive energy, and it will be a...because no entity can resist! And we will swarm upon you like love sunshine, and it will be a glorious day that all will remember."

Hybrid Children channeled by Ray Heitman 9/18/25

Connecting with the Hybrid Children is important for a couple of reasons. The first is that it really lifts you up spiritually and vibrationally and helps prepare your body to receive higher vibrational energies. The second reason is more esoteric, but maybe more important. Connecting with the Hybrid Children, or extraterrestrials, helps anchor more of that higher vibrational energy into our environment and the Earth's electromagnetic grid, which means each new contact and interaction with them helps to raise the vibration of the entire planet.

You do not have to wait until they come to Earth to connect with them, as channeling, automatic writing, telepathy, and dream connections are possible. For me, I was connecting with them for about six months before they asked to be channeled, but my connection started with me inviting them into my channeling process. It took time, but each interaction with them made the next one easier and strengthened the communication bond between us. It was easy and joyous. More like flexing connective muscles or warming up a voice before singing, and my body naturally became more accustomed to their energy. The Future Pleiadians I channel assisted in that process after several months had passed, like they were waiting for that channeling link connection with the Hybrid Children to unfold. Looking back, I believe that was part of the plan all along.

As noted, your own connection to the Hybrid Children does not have to result in channeling. When you are in a relaxed meditative state, ask for them to come in and verbally say, "I am open." Be excited about the prospect of connecting with them. By doing so, you hit all the necessary points for manifestations to occur in our physical reality: intent, physical action to support the intent, a belief you will do so, and an emotional connection. The only things that could stand in your way are: conflicting beliefs and doubts like "I can't do this," "It's not for me," "It's hard," fears of unworthiness, what will others think, it's evil, or a lack of effort. The stronger the emotion, the faster the manifestation. Have a pen and paper or recording device handy when you do this to just write down or say whatever comes to you. That is also a very good way to make a connection to your higher self or other beings who may wish to come to you and maybe through you in automatic writing or vocal channeling.

Each year, I estimate about 100,000 new channelers awaken to their gifts, and now there are millions of them spread across the globe. There have been almost ten in just our High Vibe Channeling group itself. Each new channeler is anchoring energy to raise the vibration of the Earth Collective, as well as gaining more information and insights that may not otherwise be available to them or to those who participate in their sessions. I find my channeling connections and the information and wisdom that come through in those sessions highly valuable. It has greatly increased my personal vibrational frequency, opened many avenues for even greater expansion, and given me access to even greater fields of information. It has enabled relationships to foster and grow, helped me become a better mentor and Teacher, and put me in touch with dozens of nonhuman entities who are willing to share their perspectives and love with me. The only downside for me is that I do not have endless time to channel and communicate with our "fans." Tasks due to living in this 3-D reality get in the way of my passions to experience more of the love and wonder that emanate from those connections. With the Hybrid Children being but one example.

With the current high-vibrational global climate frequency we are experiencing, I believe any adult willing to connect will be able to do so. You need only be authentic and clear away the impediments and low-vibrational behaviors. Would you like to connect directly with the Hybrid Children? They have told me and our High Vibe Channeling group in October of 2025 that anyone who channels will now be able to channel them. Any entity channeling the Hybrid Children will love them and be happy to help coordinate that connection. They are very excited about the prospect of connecting with more and more humans, and I know of several other channelers who now bring them in as well. I am excited too! Here is that message in their own words.

"We are so excited. It seems that we are going to be spreading our awareness through other channelers. It has come to the vibrational equivalent of an open door in some ways for a, for a great or a significant number of individuals on your planet. And although this is a special connection which we have with you (Uncle Ray), there are many such connections, for it is part of our mission. It is part of the overall plan. And the more love that we can inject into your collective, then the sooner we get to come and be with you in person in a more physicalized fashion."

Hybrid Children channeled by Ray Heitman 10/10/25
https://www.youtube.com/watch?v=1hESjy7g5Ig&t=26s

One more aspect of channeling the Hybrid Children channelers may not be aware of is that a new sense is being awakened. That is the interconnectedness of those who channel the Hybrid Children, as each is in touch with higher energies and realms which exist beyond our physical scope. At that "level," all things are shared and can be known simply by focusing upon them, which is merely matching the frequency at which they exist. In that way, each channeler is connected not only to beings who possess that grander perspective but also to beings who can help aid the transmission of information between those who are connected to that majestic, ever-expanding field of information. With the knowing that that field of information exists, coupled with the belief we can and do tap into it, and the belief we can connect to all consciousness through it, humans will usher in a new blending of the minds into the unified consciousness. That has never been experienced in the history of the grand experiment we call Earth. All aspects of that achievement are coming into realization, slowly at first, as things must unfold at the speed at which we are able to accept and integrate them. What we are calling channeling today will become a normal occurrence in several generations, but you don't have to wait. We are already aware when someone is staring at us, or someone close to us is thinking about us. This is just another extension of those gifts and the awakening of that "sense" in human terms. The Hybrid Children remarked on it this way:

"And we are looking forward to branching out even further and further. And that will happen too. And you are part of that. And others are part of that. And it is all a...in ways a tele-connective network which is being developed amongst all of those who channel. So you may be able to have connection with others who channel us, because we will have that connection. And you can have that connection through us because we are in telempathic connection with all of those beings. It is, um, in some ways, what you would consider a workaround. But it is still an important development. And it is one of your burgeoning senses which you are developing, even if you are not aware of it. So we will let that little cat out of the bag."

Hybrid Children channeled by Ray Heitman 10/21/25
https://youtu.be/qq-NaeXxLl0

And that connective consciousness will extend beyond humans and extraterrestrials alike and will include many of the larger creatures on our planet. They shared more on that process of working with the larger mammals on our planet to help them enable that ability, to help them biologically, so their bodies can handle that energy. They talk about it here:

"We will go back to our studies and our connections, our mental, not intrusions, but our mental explorations into those big cats. We've already done pretty much...well, the cetaceans have always been in contact with us, but we have already done your elephants and other things, and we are working on this in a systematic way. And it is more by species than by region. And even the ones in your zooooos and your compounds in that way, um, they will be focuses of this type of lesson as well. Because all of those big cats...you will not...the way you keep those animals will change. And the way you nurture and protect those animals will change. It will be a more comprehensive plan and execution...not execution in the killing...and in the fulfillment of those plans."

Hybrid Children channeled by Ray Heitman 1/18/26
    https://youtu.be/w7RzB1Ypf-M

If channeling is not your thing, you can always connect with them in the dream state, but be advised that is not the preferred way they choose to connect because when they connect more directly they not only build useful connections with humans which may prove to be beneficial after they arrive to Earth, but they directly raise the vibration of those individuals and to anchor more high vibrational energy into the Earth. And by raising the vibration of humans, that energy can then ripple out like an epidemic of love, which does not happen in dream state contacts. I never fully understood that difference until I asked them. They address the difference in this quote.

"We understand your question about the dream states and how to best connect with us there. And, you already know all the answers for that. It depends on your intent. And it depends on your openness and your dream suggestions. But the other part is not so apparent. It is the necessity for doing so from our end. And that is not our main purpose, our chosen way of...of connecting. And it is not the way chosen for us by the other entities which are involved in Open Contact. So you can do so, you can do so! But the best way, the way we wish to come through, is through the channeling states or the relaxation or the meditation, where we can connect in that way and connect to you telempathically. That is more of a benefit for us because that is a way where we can inject more of our energy into not only those particular beings who want to be joyously amped up like yourself, but to anchor more of that energy within your Earth realm as well. And when we do that, it opens up that pathway of connection. So once we do get planet siiiiiide, then we will have those connections already. And we can help surge that energy through and help raise the resonant...the frequency vibration of all of the individuals who are around those individuals who are already connected with us. That is a very helpful thing."

Hybrid Children channeled by Ray Heitman 1/18/26
   https://youtu.be/w7RzB1Ypf-M

If you wish to attempt to connect with them in the dream state, it is a fairly simple process. While you are in bed, give yourself sleep suggestions that you would like to connect with the Hybrid Children and remember that contact, and be excited about doing so. And, of course, believe you will! You may find that keeping a dream journal and pen next to your bed to write down your dreams helps provide the physical action to help that manifestation take place. The Hybrid

Children said they will answer those calls, but if you don't remember, do not get frustrated, as that will help form a barrier to that connection. I personally have many dream interactions with ETs, and quite a few of my dreams feature small children, but I cannot say whether they were Hybrid Children. They have commented before they have visited me in dreams, but I have not remembered, so I know it happens. At least I have my telempathic and channeling connections to spend time with the little darlings who reside in my heart.

"Thank you alllll for supporting us with your love and your attention and for being with us on this journeyyyyy. And may weeeee connect with you not only in dreamsssssss, but in sacred places where we can meet and clasp hands in friendship and in love."

Hybrid Children channeled by Ray Heitman 6/8/25
https://www.youtube.com/watch?v=oevNOlFzpuQ&t=8s

Another aspect of connecting with the Hybrid Children is more literal: obtaining information about whether you are a parent of a hybrid child. I personally have two: a young boy about eight and a young girl about thirteen, information I received from channeled entities. They are part of the group of children who may come forth in my channeling, as they switch off who gets to take the stage, I will say. Per the entity Ajax, channeled by Chris Blake, I have donated about 23% of their biological makeup. I wonder if I will recognize any of my traits or biology in them. I did ask the Future Pleiadians about determining who was a DNA donor to a hybrid child and about the names they choose, and this is what they had to say:

"The names of the Hybrid Children are those things which have relevance to the particular parents. Things which elicit a certain threshold of joy in those who have donated some of their DNA to those endeavors and have enabled those creations to and to have an

attachment to them. Now, for your particular case, you have already received some information of them of the two Hybrid Children which you are connected to, and many of the other ones which you are connected to but not in such a straightforward biological manner. And the honey is quite the apropos name for one of them. And the other one has a combination of names, but it is of a leaf. And we will leave that to you. Or let them come forth with that themselves."

Future Pleiadians channeled by Ray Heitman 1/30/26

https://www.youtube.com/watch?v=bG9L0xpgCh8&t=1s

"And as for your second question about how do humans understand or know that they have Hybrid Children, that is not so straightforward. For in certain instances, the higher selves would prefer that those beings, their offspring in ways in manifesting into the physical realm, are not aware that they even have them. But for others, it is a pleasant gift to understand that they have contributed to the succeeding generations by coming forth in that way to have what they truly consider to be their offspring. And they love them already innately. And while there is a wide disparity in that, the truth is, you can feel that connection when you hear the term hybrid child. What does it stir within you? That is the important discernment. Of course, your beliefs have a lot to do with that. For if you do not believe it is possible, then your ego will prohibit in many ways, or at least not form a barrier, but impede that information from reaching your consciousness. So there is no straightforward answer to that other than using your own discernment, and obviously, in a meditative state, it will be easier for you to obtain that information or any human who is open to receiving that information. For in those instances, such as right when you awaken from sleep, your ego is not fully engaged. We will say, and it is easier for information to slip in and become part of your awareness."

Future Pleiadians channeled by Ray Heitman 1/30/26

https://www.youtube.com/watch?v=bG9L0xpgCh8&t=1s

More on their naming and feeling their energy from Zariyah…

"The flood of creative, imaginative capacity or capability that you felt in that moment is the energy of the Hybrid Children. You recognize that they do embody not just that imaginative power that is typical of childhood, but also that creative beauty that is typical of nature. And it is that reason, for that reason, that they are often named after aspects of nature. Be they flowers or plant life or elemental components. And therefore, wherever you are able to lull yourself into that powerful vibrational space of creativity and imagination, you are within the bandwidth of the Hybrid Children. Know that your efforts to call them in have not gone unheard, they were indeed responded to almost immediately. And this is how the introduction of the Hybrid Children will be initialized in your civilization. It will be a yearning or an excitement coming forth from human beings to engage with the Hybrid Children. And by pulsating out a vibrational frequency range that is resonant with the vibrational frequency signature of the Hybrid Children such as creativity and imagination, that is how you will lay that foundation of communication that you will find the more you practice the more will grow."

Zariyah channeled by Aisling O'Donnell 9/12/24

https://www.youtube.com/watch?v=N5CKXySjJ7Y

Chapter Eight

The Hybrid Children as Christ Consciousness

You may have noticed, but most likely you haven't, the similarities between the Hybrid Children and the Christ Consciousness. I am not talking so much about Jesus Christ himself, but the abilities, unconditional love, and energies he possessed and provided to those he encountered. Many individuals are waiting for the return of the Christ, which happens about every 2,000 years. Now, I concede the Christ in the Bible is merely a representation, and it is doubtful any part of the Bible is an accurate reflection of actual events which occurred, but the divine energy from which Christianity sprung from is very real indeed, and the unadulterated book would have told a very different story from the abridged and altered version pushed upon and relied upon by religious followers today. Let's look beyond the myths within it and look at the similarities between the Christ Consciousness and the Hybrid Children.

1) Both are very high-vibrational beings. Christ vibrated about 300,000 cps, very close to the 333,000 cps boundary where nonphysical or spirit exists above it and energy manifests as physical below it, just like the Hybrid Children. That enables all who encounter them to feel the love, as each person encountering Jesus or the Hybrid Children could not help but to have their vibration increased. That vibration also allows them both to interact with spirit-level beings, to foresee events from our past and future, and to view our energetic

forms outside of spirit to know our true intents and beliefs, regardless of what we may communicate.

2) Messages. Both urged others to be like them. To exhibit unconditional love for all things. To seek a connection to the higher realms, and to respect, love, and honor all beings on the planet and the planet itself. That means all beings or forms of consciousness who are different from us. They also urged us to protect the planet, help those in need, love thy neighbor, abstain from violence, and there are other messages of a similar vein which they have in common. The Hybrid Children do not view them as sins, and I doubt Jesus did either. That is a label humans made up to try to goad or motivate followers into conformity, which followed human beliefs, and not a higher realm. But gluttony, coveting, greed, envy, and wrath are all things of which neither approve. Other "sins" of sloth, lust, and pride are human tenets made up by humans to get them to conform to the views of the ruling few and do not come from the heart, but the mind. The others are focused on acceptance, love, and taking care of one's divine bodily form, not on control, which is a good indicator of whether a guideline comes from the heart or a higher calling, or from the mind and mankind.

3) Setting examples for us to follow. None of us can hope to do better than to emulate the unconditional love and joy of the Hybrid Children or Jesus. They not only speak directly of those things, but practice them in how they live their life. They urge us to be the best we can by showing us their authentic selves and informing us of the practices that can make us more like them, by aligning ourselves with the call of love from which we came.

4) Attracting others. Just as Jesus did, the Hybrid Children will create a huge following, as anyone who comes into contact with them will form a loving attachment to them. They change people and create a desire to experience more of the unconditional love they have to offer.

5) They came to teach us. The Hybrid Children are coming to the planet to show us a better way to live and to help us resolve the issues we have created in our societies and on our planet. To work with other beings to form a loving world where all beings have a chance to thrive, and where resources and laws support all and not just the few who know how to manipulate them through immoral means they claim as their right. The Hybrid Children will help us turn the tables on those who desire to keep us imprisoned within old systems. Sound familiar?

6) Creation. Neither was conceived by humans through normal reproductive means, and the term immaculate was chosen to differentiate the biological creation which was chosen for our physical expression. The fact is, the Hybrid Children and Jesus were both created artificially by nonhumans to be a bridge from where we are to where we could be, and both were designed and created specifically for the roles they were to take on their Earthly missions.

The return of the Christ Consciousness timing aligns with the arrival of the Hybrid Children on our Earth within the next five years. And when the truth comes out about the religious and power structures that have been manipulated for centuries, humanity will cast them down and build anew. Jesus was not able to get the job done. The vibrational difference between the people of his day was too great to take hold and spread across the globe, but the Hybrid Children will spread across the globe literally and figuratively. They will bring their loving vibration to uplift and bring change where it is needed. And like in Jesus's time, there will be factions which act against them because there will be those who wish to preserve the status quo, but this time they will fail. The time for change is upon us, and those who preach division, hate, and "enemies" are gasping their last breath, and they can feel their time is coming to an end. It scares them. Millions and millions are feeling a unity and hope building, which has not been able to become widespread in the history of mankind.

I am going to share a bit of what the Hybrid Children said on their session from 12/25/25, when they spoke of celebrating the energy of Christmas.

"We are here to learn and to share and to love and to teach every other being to do that too. And speaking of lovely beings and loving beings, today is a day on your planet when many people gather to celebrate your Christmas and other holidays as well. But we understand that few people understand that they are celebrating energy! It is not a human per se, but it is an ideal that they are celebrating, because that energy, that Christ energy which came to you, was meant to show humans how they could be if, if they followed those guidelines and could connect with spirit on a regular basis. Because their vibration would be so high that it would be easy to tap into the spirit realm, and that's what that gentleman Jesus did. And it was the energy, though, not the human. That's what humans kind of missed the boat on what we will say, because that energy is within us as well, and it is within you, it is within everything. And that is where pursuing your passions and vibing up and having the highest vibration you can and living a heart-full life where your heart leads in every decision that you make. That was the "turn the other cheek," because you knew it was yourself. That was that lesson, because we are all one.

"But it has become a commercialized mess in some ways, because it creates a lot of waste paper. And people spend a lot of things on things. And it is nice that they care for others, and they go out of their way to make sure that they get what people believe that they need, but there are so many others who don't get what they need. So it is not, and it's not supposed to be, a proper distribution of goods and wealth, but it...that would be nice. That would be an even better Christmas gift on your planet. So work that out for us, and we will teach you how when we get in. And it will not be that hard then, because there will be a lot more people coming around and waking up to the love within their hearts and matching it with the love within our hearts. And that

is a great connection. It is not so much the minds. It is the heart connections which really matter. And with your Christ consciousness, that's what it was all about. It was about being nice and taking care of everyone, everything. But those words, they sure did get jumbled as your time unfolded and went on, but you guys all know that. And we are here to make some corrections, if you will. To do some um, editing on your past history remembrance, as it was jotted down in all of those sacred books. And that is a fun thing for us, too, because we love teaching. Teaching and learning and sharing and loving. That wraps up our whole family crest right there.

"And so we will come down to you and remind you of the Christ energy. We will bring that with us in our little knapsacks, and we will unload it and set it on the table in front of you and say, 'This is how you could be.' And then we will jump on the table and say, 'Tadahhh! We were kidding because this is US! This is how you can be.' And it will be a marvelous awakening all over your planet, but it will not happen at once. It has to...um, it has to ripple out, and those ripples take some time. But that's okay, for all you need to do is utilize as much of that Christ energy as you can, to think like a hybrid child, act like a hybrid child. And then you will be much, much closer, and your vibration will go up, up, up, so you can bring us in sooner and connect with us more fully."

The Hybrid Children channeled by Ray Heitman 12/25/25
https://youtu.be/x-lzzWTN8Jc

As you can see, they are already aware they were created to bring the Christ Consciousness Energy back to Earth, and they will not be dissuaded from that mission. And it will ripple across the Earth, just like they said. Now, let's look at the Christ Consciousness of around 2,000 years ago. The entity Zariyah, channeled by Aisling O'Donnell, offers a little perspective on those events from her broader view in her 12/23/23 session titled "Following Yonder Star."

"Greetings, this is Zariyah from the Orion civilization. We are so pleased that you have joined with us at this festive time of year for a brief transmission. Today, we will discuss the Christmas story and the importance of the Bethlehem star. Like most mythologies in your public discourse, the story of the birth of Christ is a metaphor that can be interpreted many ways. That is not to say that Yeshua was not a real person on your planet Earth. However, there is many more surprises included into the story for those who like unwrapping presents at this time of the year. The Bethlehem star was the star that guided the wise kings to the birthplace of Christ, and well, they were looking at the stars because the stars are from whence the hybrid program began. Your Virgin Mary, as she is often referred to, was Immaculate indeed, but the immaculate part that is referred to when we speak of the Virgin Mary is her vibration. Her vibration was immaculate, so she could participate in one of the significant hybrid births on your Earth. If you understand the term Elohim in the Hebrew Bible, the Elohim represent different factions of different ET species who came to augment the Homo sapien as they were originally imagined by upgrading their DNA into a more advanced, more enlightened being.

"This program was often done through the birthing process in what you might consider a miraculous birth, and this miraculous birth is usually representative of not just a being who is an avatar, who is touched somehow by the divine, but a being that represents the upgraded hybrid from the Homo sapien. Therefore, Mary needed to make her vibration immaculate in order to co-create Yeshua with the Elohim. The Elohim being represented by the angel Gabriel. All of the archangels—Gabriel, Michael, Sophriel—these are all representative of different strands of the Elohim, different strands of the impregnation of your hybrid program on your planet if you can imagine that. And therefore, the story is in many ways accurate, but it hides a deeper meaning. It is not necessarily the birth of the savior onto Earth, but the upgrading of the human being's potential so that they could, in fact, have access to knowledge of their capabilities and

potentials and of their true nature, which is a fractal of Source. It is also a profound guidance for the times that you now find yourselves in, because you are trying to achieve that vibration of contact. The window is open now, and it is important, as we have in many transmissions now suggested to you, to keep raising your vibration in order to reach that 222,000 cycles per second for Open Contact.

"If you can imagine, Mary herself was an avatar of vibrational raising capabilities, as was her mother Anna an avatar of vibrational raising capabilities. It was her that taught Mary how to do that. And in her having the immaculate vibrational frequency range she was able to have contact with, in this case Elohim, an Anunnaki faction and bring through Yeshua. How exciting. Therefore, the present we would offer you this Christmas is to recognize that at every moment you have a new opportunity to give birth to a higher vibrational frequency. And that, as you give birth to this higher vibrational frequency range, you get closer and closer to contact. If you can make contact, you can unlock some of the locked capabilities in your DNA strand and essentially give birth to yourself as the true Homo galacticus that you seek to become. The Christmas story is not just about some religious Messiah. It is about the giving birth to the true human race that you all have potentially locked inside you. And so we encourage you to celebrate, yes, the birth of Yeshua the hybrid, because you are in fact all descendants of hybrid programs, but also to celebrate Mary the instructress in achieving the vibrational frequency range of contact."

Zariyah channeled by Aisling O'Donnell 12/23/23

https://www.youtube.com/watch?v=jMR6iB8GKCw&t=25s

I find that session transcript interesting and exciting indeed. It is the story that is before us now. The new world we are creating is because the time is right, and we are ripe for lasting change. It will unify the planet and all consciousness upon it in ways that you cannot imagine, but it will happen. It will slowly take hold, and then the shift that has been talked about for years will take place. The return of the Christ Consciousness is not the return of Jesus himself, although do not be surprised if that energy again takes place in human form, the form of the Hybrid Children. *And The Children Shall Lead Us.*

Now let's take a look at the other beings who are guiding, supporting, and loving us to help us get to where we are going—our galactic neighbors. Those beings who are the foundation of Open Contact and those who will interact with us further in our future, once we are ready.

Chapter Nine

Meet Our Galactic Neighbors

" And so that is being looked upon and rejoiced by other galactic beings who are not Hybrid Children but from different races, that you (Ray) are so open with the Hybrid Children. Opening your heart and your own personal home with the Hybrid Children, that we are learning from this relationship. And we want you to understand what great work you are doing and recognize that within yourself."

Divine Crystalline Collective
channeled by Isabelle Rohach Zimmerman 1/1/26
   https://youtu.be/Oc3tXIFXrw4

While there are millions and millions of beings interested in and observing the transformation of humanity into a more loving and less dense form, and while there are extraterrestrial representatives and attributes of almost all species on our planet from bugs to whales, there are a handful which are more intimately involved in the continued progress of humanity in a more hands-on basis and helping to empower the Open Contact event. They are the Lyrans, Yahyel, Andromedans, and Pleiadians. There are also many other beings which have direct or supporting roles, such as the Sassani. This chapter will help others get an overview of the main players humanity will be interacting with freely in another thirty to fifty years.

In writing this book, I am fortunate to get information directly from the Hybrid Children and other beings I channel and encounter in sessions, as well as being guided by other beings as to when to write or stop writing. While I know that may sound strange to those who do not allow their intuition to lead them as they navigate their physical world, as I do, it is how I have lived for more than thirty-five years. During my metaphysical journey, I have learned a lot about many extraterrestrial races, but I found that I did not have a grasp on who the major players in Open Contact were or how they fit together to create the overall mission. I asked a group of entities in a High Vibe Channeling session on 1/18/26 and was told there were busloads of Andromedans, eight groups from the Pleiades, four distinctive ones from Lyra, and the Yahyels who served as Teachers to the Hybrid Children. That was a great start, but I found I still needed to research each of those to get the details I needed. Then inspiration hit me, and I decided to ask the Hybrid Children about them all, but changed my mind and decided to ask the Future Pleiadians I channel instead. I am so glad I did, as I would not have found that information anywhere else, and I am sincerely grateful for their help. This is what they had to say about the major players of Open Contact in their own words, and again, you can find this video on the High Vibe Channeling YouTube channel. It is quite a long and informative quote, and the information they provided was all new to me.

"And we thank you for reaching out to us in your reasonably called 'time of need' to secure more information on the major players who are involved in Open Contact, as well as indirectly in the ascension of humanity. You must understand this is a long-term project. Thousands of your years have gone into the makings of this event. And we and ours in our lineage have been part of that for quite some time, being Future Pleiadians as you know us, and we have an overall role in coordination ourselves. Now, our particular bent on this in your terms is to obtain all of those perspectives on Open Contact for our own personal benefit, so we may form some 'closure,' is a term which you are familiar with. And view the entire thing from

beginning to end as far as this chapter goes, for the chapters are still being written. Filled out page by page, and will continue until you, too, your race, has evolved into a non-physical form.

"For all time is revealed. All time has happened. And when you access a certain point, a certain vibrational level, although it is not that simplistic, it is more of a knowing, an encapsulating, and not even an integrating. For you do not need to hold that information within you. You merely have to know the frequencies which will bring it to you. And while that sounds like a, the same thing or similar in your ways, it can only be viewed as such. But there are many, many nuances and many complexities and challenges which must be handled or overcome in order to obtain that perspective.

"Now, our particular brothers and sisters of the Pleiadian's star systems have had a direct role in this from the Roswell incident. You will say not that they were directly the aliens which were asked to be the subjects found in those starships. But in mentoring many of your kind throughout your history, they are indeed extremely loving beings, and they shied away from those who would corrupt that power, but they did have their hands within it. Many of the speakers which you know of and those which you follow have had the influence of the Pleiadians within them. They provide a loving touch, a hand to guide and stabilize and steady those paths, those threads of energy which weave through your generations. And that, in a general way, is their role, and that will continue to be their role. And while the differentiations between them are many and not for human consumption at this time, it is not necessary. You have not attained sufficient knowledge in order to appreciate and interact with them on a fuller basis, but yet they have the courage to come forth and show you and be in front of you. In that way, they are courageous. And they know their role, and they are excellent at it, and their love will persevere. And we will let that go for that aspect of this revelation of knowledge related to that fine book which you are assembling.

"Now the Andromedans are more the powerhouse which propels all of us because their energy is vast, their knowledge is vast. And while they are not prone to niceties in your terms, they are indeed loving in their own way. And because this was such a novel endeavor, they wholeheartedly chose and volunteered themselves to be involved in the creation of your planet, in the creation of many of your beings. In a supporting role to allow those other sections, those other races, those other energies to be able to have their input felt within it. And because this is their 'baby' in ways which you term, which is rather analogous and not at all appropriate, but it, it, they have a special place in their heart for this. For this entire transformation. And they are coming to many, many, many on your planet, as they have come to you. They have been waiting in ways for humans to attain the wherewithal, the courage, yes, that word again, and the vibrational capacity so they can interact on a freer basis. And their role…well, they will not be among you in the first several generations after Open Contact. Because of their strength, because of their might. And if they choose to do so, they may. But their role is more after the Great Reset you have learned of, for then they will be able to interact with all on your planet on a free basis, and they can change forms at their whim and still carry that signature frequency you shall know them by. They can let you, provide you with examples of how grand you can be, of the abilities you can attain. And they do not flaunt those. They merely wish for you to keep those in mind so that you may continue to reach higher and reach beyond the stars to the energies behind them. They are welcome guides and are appreciated greatly, and although they do mock humans in some ways, it is to keep your interest and to be more personable, for there is no maliciousness in them. However, they are selfish in ways. In good ways, for it serves them, and they serve many. Let the fact that they serve many be the framework you interpret them as. And we thank you for asking for our help again.

"The Lyrans are a wonderful, wonderful ancient energy which does not approve of or sanction or participate in conflict. They have no need to. They, too, have great power, but they use it in a subliminal

or subtle way. They urge, they guide, they never demand. They accept. And they will wait as they have waited for all of the time that your planet has been in existence, but they reach out to many races. They have their so-called 'fingers' in many developing societies. Like the master baker who is helping his students, telling them add a little bit here, maybe a little bit longer. Does this taste right to you? They are always sampling and urging those individuals and those societies and planetary systems to reflect on where they are and where they would like to go, and the changes that they will need to get there. And they are more than willing to help. But you will find that they prefer that you learn those lessons yourself. That you accept their guidance and see where it goes. To see those results and take ownership of them. That is one of the reasons why humans have to be shown and have to be reasoned with, and why no one is going to give you all of the answers. It would not serve you. And that is their influence. And that is their influence in why you are, humans are, the way you are. Because you do not take stuff for granted, because there is a part of you that wants to know the backstory, that does not want the simple answers, that wants to figure it out. And that is a main role in your densified reality. For outside of it, all is known. There are still challenges, and when we say that, know that it is not that there are not secrets in that way, but there are not. But it is just an expansion and ability to hold, and not to manipulate, and not to integrate, but to form and reform from the information which is available, which helps to expand and forms the challenges of those particular races.

"Now, the Yahyel, as you know, are superb at matching humanity in many ways. Partly due to their being related to you. And they take special care of your precious Hybrid Children and other beings on your planet and guide them. They are indeed a very loving race. And although they are all perfect in their ways, the Yahyels are closer related to you, not only in appearance, but in genetic makeup. And while they are physicalized, they are striving towards that day and time and epoch, epoch in your ways, which they will not be physicalized. And they have many beings which are helping them

because they are such a loving and interesting species. And they are indeed the caretakers, the nurturers, and the guides, and the masters, not in the way of control, and the supreme Teachers of the Hybrid Children. And they are deeply loving. Deeply loving. And they care for them greatly. And that love, that bond, is reflected in the relationships between them and the other hybrid races, including the Hybrid Children. And they indeed have experimented in ways and chosen the best ways and individuals and groups and races and species to administer part of learnings which are required for the Hybrid Children's lessons. So they are the orchestrators in ways of, not so much their creation, although they have a hand in that, but in their educational system. They have devised how and when they will develop and guide them through the phases and the processes which have been carefully chosen by the heart energy, we will say. That is their role. They are masterful at it. And they wish to love you more. And they really look forward to coming in and having those personal interactions with humans. And they have been silent for the most part to let others who are more experienced in those ways have their efforts to come first. It is the natural flow of things. It is not that one is better than another. It is choosing the right tool, the right energy for the right situation. And when their time comes, they will be integrating amongst you and laughing and sharing in your unified consciousness and touching your hearts as well. And while yes, there are many other races which are involved, we are going to end this little lesson here for you."

The Future Pleiadians channeled by Ray Heitman 1/19/26

https://youtu.be/m-D-tnbtzA4

While there are many civilizations participating in Open Contact, one important race, also known as the third hybrid race, is the Sassani. They have many roles, like the aptly named First Contact Specialists, as they have helped hundreds of different races transform themselves into galactic, spacefaring partners who are now members of a very large group known as the Cosmic Alliance, which has over 167,000 different races of beings in it. Bashar and Elan are two well-known Sassani ambassadors who have been in contact with humans via channeling for decades. You may think of the Sassani as very experienced and capable event coordinators, stage managers, or orchestra conductors who ensure everything occurs in its proper sequence, in the proper form, at the proper time, so everything flows and the event/performance goes off without a hitch. They are loving, quasi-physical beings who live a life of synchronicity and wish to see humans achieve the more unified, loving beings we are capable of, which is why they have chosen to fulfill the roles they have in Open Contact. In my understanding, all contact events flow through them to make sure they conform to established mission protocols. I also asked the Future Pleiadians about the Sassani. This is what they had to say…

"And we thank you once again for coming to us for more information. More directly from the source, we will say, on the Sassani, Sassani interactions and roles with humanity in regards to Open Contact. They are the ones who initially propose the idea, and they are the orchestrators of the Open Contact. And they are working with the other species and races and coordinating them in ways for each, although they flow in their own natural ways. There are organizational details which must be handled and integrated into a cohesive whole, and that is their role. They are indeed 'point men,' you would say, in this operation. And not so much that they are directly involved with the humans themselves, other than through the channeling and providing information and building awareness. And their coordination skills are unparalleled in this, for their experiences shall lead them. And the glimpses that humans get of them are a small fraction of a percentage of their total abilities and their impacts on other roles in galactic societies. While we would not say that they are the major players, they are the ones who are coordinating everything

after it has been set in motion. And we hope that that distinction comes through, for they are indeed vital to this. It would not happen without them. And we all appreciate and love their guidance and their experiences which they bring forth into that guidance.

"And while we were on the subject, yes, there are many other races who are involved in this, but you have had us come forth for all of the ones which are most significant. Now, each has its own particular role. Each being, each species, each race, and each member of those races have their own desires and fulfillment and needs in that way for coming forth and interacting with humans, as we do. This is a mixed bag with many different agendas, goals, desires, fulfillments, explorations beyond what anyone on your planet in human form could ever entail or seek to comprehend in any way of a fullness, a comprehensive overall understanding. In summary, just understand that it is many ingredients going into baking this cake of humanity. And they come from a wide variety of locations, origins, and the energies which they bring forth all contribute to the final product. And it will be a tasty morsel indeed. And you may decorate it how you wish, for humans are indeed setting the temperature to determine how long this particular brand of bakery goods cooks. And we go with love, and we recede."

Future Pleiadians channeled by Ray Heitman 1/22/26

https://www.youtube.com/watch?v=aJWAlbFh_CU&t=2s

Some of the other beings involved in Open Contact, I shall just name here, and if you feel the impulse to learn more about them, please do so, as I find all of them very interesting. They include the Greys, Arcturians, Sirians, Tall Whites, Reptilians, Mantis beings, Insectoids, and what have been called the Inner Earth beings, which may include some of the previously listed races. There is a lot of information out there on them, but some of it is sensationalized, so use your discernment. This list does not include the more "native" nonhuman beings on our planet, such as Sasquatch and elementals, which are a wide variety of energies of the wind, air, fire, water, earth, and inner Earth, and the wee folk (faeries, sprites, etc.) also have parts to play. These beings are not superstition nor fantasy, and those who believe in them were ridiculed and chided for centuries, but there is a reason those stories persist, and after Open Contact, more will be revealed about them. The cetacean nation (whales and dolphins) also has a role to play. And while those beings and the other extraterrestrials are not the main focus of this book, please understand they are all loving entities who are observing and interacting with humans, and many of them are being channeled by individuals.

Not all extraterrestrial races assume a physical presence or shape. In addition, there are many groups of nonphysical entities, including various councils, oversoul groups, and higher-mind collectives, which are not races per se, but which do support, guide, and observe humanity and the beings involved. I am connected with at least three of those groups. The Usol, who are a humorous group whose name is a bad pronunciation of "us all." The YOU beings, who are powerful entities that stress our own manifestation powers. And finally, Sseneno, which is oneness spelled backwards. The actual number of beings and races involved in our planet and its transformation is more than we can imagine or know, but please remember one thing—they are part of the love story of humanity's transformation and are not to be feared, but understood and accepted, like all consciousness on our planet.

One group of extraterrestrials, which are important to know but have not been touched upon much except for the Sassani, is the other five hybrid races. I will summarize them, but their stories are interesting and play a part in the creation of the Hybrid Children as well. I will present them in the order in which they were created according to their progression, as each previous version was utilized to help create the next batch, kind of like a sourdough starter in ways. These are simplified explanations, and if you are interested, I urge you to dig deeper into their histories. The terms and concepts used in this section may not be ones you are familiar with, but you can always learn more about them later if that is the case for you. The time scales of these achievements are not included, but can be hundreds and hundreds of years. Most of this information is from the videos of Bashar channeled by Darryl Anka, who has been providing valuable information for over forty years.

The first hybrid race is known as the Maz'eh. They were created from human and DNA from a race called the "Greys." The Greys are the most common characterization of extraterrestrials with large heads and eyes and slight torsos and limbs compared to modern-day humans. They are genetic specialists, but had to learn their lessons the hard way, it seems. Their society chose technological advancement over emotion, and, per my understanding, altered their DNA to the point where they had very little or no emotions at all. Unfortunately, part of the changes they made to the DNA made them unable to reproduce, so they reached out to humans to cultivate and create new beings so they could live on in those beings. Those sourcings of human DNA are the catalyst of many abduction myths, as the Greys did not understand their actions would cause fear, as they did not feel or understand emotions, although the humans involved were not harmed biologically and approved of their genetic donations on a higher realm level.

The new race they created from a mix of their DNA and ours was called the Maz'ani or Mazani. The Maz'ani are known as the "Tall Greys." They are the second hybridization involving human DNA, but neither of the first two hybrid races created were sufficient to carry on their genetic line, so they tried again, and the Sas'sani or Sassani mentioned previously were created. They are known as the third hybrid race and are a balance of approximately half Grey and half human DNA. They have progressed to the point where they are vibrationally designated as quasi-physical beings, meaning they possess both physical and nonphysical characteristics. For instance, they do not have blood in their bodies but utilize nonphysical energic flows instead and draw a great percentage of their energy from the etheric realm, and no longer need to consume food from external sources. They are slightly smaller than the average human and have small and slender appendages and features, but larger heads and eyes. Their skin is like fine silk and may be white to grayish.

The fourth hybrid race is the Sha'ya'el, which are more human in appearance than the Sassani, but are another progression in becoming more human in appearance. They still have larger eyes, but are not as slender as the Sassani and look enough like humans to pass among us. They are the so-called guides and organizers of the fifth hybrid race, the Ya'ya'el, or Yahyel, as mentioned previously. The Sha'ya'el will assist the Yahyel in preparing for their missions in Open Contact.

Because the Yahyel are more representative of us in appearance, they can and do pass among humans without notice. They are fourth-density beings, and because they appear to be human, they will be the first hybrid race to make contact with us. They will be able to interact with those of us who have raised their vibrational frequency enough to safely do so. They are the primary Teachers of the Hybrid Children, but have many roles among them and in the Open Contact scenario.

The next hybrid race is our beloved Hybrid Children, who are known as the Sha'linya (Sha-lin-i-ya) or Shalanaya. Their name means "The First Ones" in the ancient language, per Bashar. Their role is not just to help us understand all they can be and to help us become acclimated to new technologies and extraterrestrial races, but they will blend and have biological children with humans to produce the sixth hybrid race called the E'nanni'ka or Enannika.

The Enannika are the next evolution of humanity, which can be called Homo galacticus. They will be high-vibrational beings who will be able to freely interact with most of our galactic neighbors and the spirit realm. They are not the last evolution of humanity, though, as there will be a blending of all of those hybrid races into one new race called the Anu'het or Anu Het, who will be the grand conclusion of the development of the hybridization program.

Chapter Ten

Preparing for Your Personal Contact Event

This chapter will focus on you, the reader, to help open your mind and prioritize those things that will not only assist you in your everyday life, but also beyond it. It will help give you a better idea of what to expect and enable you to make the right choices in your quest for your own extraterrestrial contact event. To help you understand the risks of not being prepared as well. Let's start with a little litmus test to help you determine where you may be now. Please take three deep breaths and center yourself, and then continue reading.

See this scene unfolding in your mind. An extraterrestrial race has officially contacted and visited Earth. Videos and headlines of spaceships hovering in our skies are being viewed across the planet. A similar spaceship silently appears before you, flowing from beneath the horizon and expanding in a timeless, silent moment, as it moves closer to you, descending softly nearby. A voice enters your mind, reassuring you, and you feel your heart beating fast and your quickening breath. This is it! The contact event you have been hoping for. A being emerges, raises a hand, and begins purposeful strides toward you. A telepathic greeting and reassurance are received in the recesses of your mind. You feel a tingle in the air and on your skin, and fight the urge to flee as excitement and anticipation win out over the survival instinct of the ego.

How did that scenario make you feel? What is your emotional reaction? Fear? Excitement? If you were able to put yourself in that place and time, your first thought when you read that question may help determine if you are a good candidate for open face-to-face alien physical contact. If your initial response is fear, anger, or disbelief, please leave contact to others until you are better acclimated to the idea and can manage your emotions to avoid engaging fight or flight reflexes. That fight or flight reflex and human unpredictability are good reasons why aliens will wait until humanity is ready before attempting contact openly. Some humans react violently when scared or confronted with the unknown, or when losing an argument. That sentiment is playfully reflected in the following quote by a Sassani First Contact Specialist called Bashar, channeled by Darryl Anka, who is well-known with millions of followers. "Why would we want to land in an insane asylum where all the inmates have guns?" For those who might respond in fear, rest assured, with their technology, they do not intend harm. If they did, would they bother meeting you first? Of course not.

As humanity heads for the first wave of "face-to-face" alien encounters in the contact year of 2027, a growing number of us appear to be good candidates for an extraterrestrial encounter, but too few to make it happen, so efforts to reach the appropriate vibrational level continue. Your personal reaction to Open Contact is one step in determining your readiness, but significant bodily and mental preparations are needed. Not only to enable contact, but to be able to have meaningful exchanges with extraterrestrials without undesired consequences.

There's an abundance of galactic neighbors who wish to meet with us. Whether you are unsure or believe it impossible or unlikely they exist, the information provided here can be of value to you by opening up endless possibilities to explore mentally. Open Contact is our future. The following sections cover the basics, and some of the material already presented will be explored in greater detail. Those sections include vibration, mental health and stability, bodily health, beliefs, the risks of not being ready, and a couple of exercises to help prepare you. Understand that you most likely already experience extraterrestrial contact in the dream state. The dream "forum" provides a way to help gauge your readiness for contact and allows our galactic friends to help guide and prepare you for the experiences that will manifest in the physical realm. You may even play with different variables in dreams for contact events to see which one "fits" for you.

To review, your vibrational frequency range corresponds to the amount of love energy our higher self is able to express moment by moment through our physical being. Our ability to experience and emanate expressions of joy and love. The more joyful you are and the less emotional "baggage" you carry, the higher frequency you're able to maintain. If you participate in low-vibrational events like gossip or drama, or harbor beliefs of fear, anger, resentment, or jealousy, your vibration will drop to match the low-vibrational event or emotion. Our galactic friends have extremely high vibrations that can be harmful for us if our vibration is too low and far away from theirs. If you want to have an Open Contact experience, it's important for you to maintain the highest vibration you can and keep allowing for expansion. If it is not safe for you, extraterrestrials are not going to attempt it. These are loving beings and do not wish for you to experience any undesired effects.

Let me explain. Your vibrational range is expressed as cycles per second (cps) in our linear Earth experience. Most humans currently average between 40,000 and 80,000cps, but are trending higher. Per Zariyah on 12/7/23, the entity channeled by Aisling O'Donnell , it requires a minimum vibrational frequency range of 222,000 cycles per second (cps) for humans to be ready for open alien contact to occur. That minimum vibratory rate is necessary to achieve a compatible middle ground for a safe encounter, as the vibrational rate of any contacting alien race may be five or ten times that of the highest vibrational rate humans can attain in physical form. For extraterrestrials to "personally" appear, the aliens must dampen their vibrational frequency rates considerably to operate within our dense physical reality. Maintaining a higher frequency range has other benefits besides enabling safe contact, as more information can be transmitted, and you will have a better connection with any being choosing to connect with you.

Mental health is elusive to categorize the related experiences. Their impact, and how they have been dealt with, is unique to each of us, but the causes, layers, and emotional depth attached to those experiences and related beliefs can be challenging to release. And if not dealt with and released, those energies frequently become stored in our bodily cells and cause issues later on, which is the only way our body can call attention to them to remind us they are there. Ingrained patterned responses may follow, creating an even greater challenge to release. Our bodies are great at handling the biological functions for which they were designed, but not so great at handling unresolved emotional issues. We aren't taught the skills to mentally process and release negative energies that are stuck in our bodies from unresolved traumas, worry, anxiety, guilt, or fears. Until those energies and beliefs are released, we will never be at our best physically or vibrationally. They act like a finger on a plucked guitar string, muting the vibration.

In fact, every single thought affects your vibrational range because our bodies react to our thoughts. There is a direct causal relationship between our thoughts and our bodily health; what we think and feel has a greater impact on who we are. Positive, hopeful outlooks can aid us immeasurably by bolstering energy, stamina, and other physiological metrics. Unfortunately, the reverse may be far more common. That is where doing your so-called "shadow work" or setting your "baggage" free comes in. They all need to be reconciled and released in order to be at your vibrational best for contact. Each issue held within us will create symptom after symptom, reminding you that you have energy-release work to do. "Triggers" evoking low-vibrational responses are indicators of beliefs or energies that do not serve you and limit your vibration.

I was taught a way to uncover and address those issues by a loving entity. It was doing an "End-of-Life Review," which is a good way to reveal past situations or interactions, even subconscious ones, so we can address them. You can ask your higher self or guides for help with this, then set aside a couple of hours to meditate and see what comes to mind. If you are triggered, a good way to release the beliefs or energies associated with those people or events is to view the "bad actors" as teachers and the events themselves as trying to teach you something. Perhaps boundaries, to follow your instincts, or other lessons you were supposed to learn are not what is important in these remembrances, but the release of the energies is. And by viewing those who caused you trauma or upset you as teachers, it is easier to understand they were broken people acting from the framework of beliefs they had not healed in themselves. Hurt people, hurt people. That perspective makes it easier to love them and forgive them. You need not like them or ever see them again, because the goal is to release that negative energy that's limiting your vibrational frequency. Left to remain trapped in your physical and energy bodies, that energy will act like a magnet and will continue to attract similar situations until you let it go. For instance, people who have fears of being yelled at ingrained in them from an early age will continue to attract that behavior until they learn the lesson, often never realizing that unreleased negative energy and false beliefs keep bringing those events to them. This lesson took me decades to understand, and the End-of-Life Review helped me understand it, so it may be a challenging lesson to learn, but you can do this. My End-of-Life Review took over two hours the first day, and then things that triggered me kept popping up for weeks. The strongest triggers come first, and then after I released all of those lesser ones, they almost stopped altogether. I still have some, like telemarketing calls I get frequently, but I am working on those.

Being your genuine, authentic self is also a great way to raise your vibration, but many people function within their perceived roles and the beliefs that accompany them. Many of us act differently depending on who we're with, where we are, and what we're doing. At home, work, or in organizations, restricting our behaviors or displaying others because of expected behavior protocols or to "keep the peace" stifles our genuine, authentic selves. You probably know how that feels. It cramps your style and stirs something inside you to release it, to speak your mind, let your voice be heard. To object to undesired behaviors like perceived lies or injustices, or to simply participate in a conversation. Authenticity, to me, is being the same person regardless of the external environment, and it comes with a sense of profound freedom. But there may be consequences for some, so do what is best for you, but it definitely raises your vibration, which is why it feels so good.

Health aspects not only affect vibrational range but also our quality of life. Being vigilant and discerning of what we let into our minds and making sure we support our biology are vital. You most likely know that consuming only the best quality organic food free of preservatives, pesticides, chemicals, and heavy processing is best for you, like drinking a gallon or more of the purest water each day. Those practices not only enhance our body's ability to handle the transformations necessary for a joyous Open Contact experience, but also help to ensure we are able to increase and maintain our vibrational range until contact occurs.

But that is only half of the story. We must also be cognizant of the information and individuals we allow into our experience, and, more importantly, how we react to them. As Wayne Dyer so eloquently put it, "Refuse to allow your well-being to be affected by anything external to yourself—not the weather, not the wars someplace on the globe, not the economy, and certainly not anyone else's decision to wallow in low energy." Understand the "news" and entertainment media have agendas other than your mental and physical health as they profit by generating content to help you form harmful emotional reactions. Their favorite weapons are the weakest of emotions: anger and fear. The key is not to react to them and to treat those events as benign. Not reacting or being concerned or offended by disasters, chaos, or misdeeds may sound callous to some, but it doesn't mean you "don't care." It means you care about yourself first and have chosen to respond differently than common social patterns, many of which are mostly ingrained patterns of responses that you need to recognize before you can change them, like worry or guilt. They are not necessary or healthy.

Choose to no longer put more energy and focus into situations which do not serve you. You won't be missing anything. As the Aspects of Love entities channeled by Kathleen Whitehead once advised a group in session: "Recognize but do not participate." Read that sentence again, learn from it, and take it to heart. If you find yourself reacting to faraway events or sad stories on TV, social media, or in conversation, tell yourself, "This is not for me," and let it go or use whatever means of releasing energy works for you. An affirmation like "I will only react to information that is relevant for me or which helps me on my path," or similar language repeated three times a day, will help strengthen your defenses against negative inputs. I personally do not watch the news and use my TV sparingly.

Beliefs are a very powerful component when preparing for Open Contact. When not in conflict with your expressed desires, when the action aligns with them, and when there is a strong emotional attachment to the desired outcome, they manifest. Being ready for your personal Open Contact event is the same. If you have beliefs that are low vibration and not aligned with the desire to experience Open Contact, they will impede the manifestation of such an event. Unconscious beliefs are the main culprit, as any qualms or misgivings about Open Contact or your worthiness will most likely quash them. Inversely, a steadfast belief that your personal Open Contact experience will not only occur but also be a beneficial, life-changing experience is a powerful affirmation to hold in your heart, enabling that focus to come to fruition. Once you have beliefs that serve you, protect them. Please keep those in your circle who are supportive updated on your progress, and hidden from those who are derisive or unbelieving. The more positive energy and excitement you can build towards your goal, the more likely it is to occur.

What happens if you have a face-to-face with an extraterrestrial and you're not ready? That depends on how close you are to being prepared for the event vibrationally, mentally, and physically, and the proximity of the encounter. Death or psychic shock are likely possibilities if you are unprepared, and we have enough babbling wards of the state, so please keep your distance if not ready. Remember, the extraterrestrials, these loving beings, are not going to interact with you unless it is safe for you to do so. There is really no need to be concerned, but humans can be stubborn, and "Hey, watch this!" has preceded many an epitaph, so let's examine why those risks exist.

First, extraterrestrials possess a much higher vibration than any human on the planet and are very energetic beings. Think of a power plant with a head, arms, and legs. You would not go hugging a live 220-volt wire, and the same principles apply here. Every thought and every nerve impulse in our body depends on electricity to function, and an encounter with energy of that magnitude may not only disrupt your bodily systems, but stop your heart as well, and overwhelm your psyche. The electrical aspects are easily understood and will not be discussed further, and if you need a lesson in what being shocked feels like, I am happy you have never had that experience. If you have, you never wish to repeat it. The energies of the extraterrestrials can be much stronger than humans are built to withstand in a low-vibrational state.

The psyche is another matter, and the loss of identity can occur if your vibration is not high enough to endure contact, as the psyche can get lost and lose its grip on reality in the presence of such powerful extraterrestrial energies and vibrations. As an example, think of two water hoses of very different pressures, one barely a trickle and the other going full blast, joining together into one stream and flowing through a single hose. The hose with the greater pressure and speed will overwhelm the weaker-pressured stream, involuntarily raising the speed (vibration) of the weaker stream to the new combined speed of their joined stream. The trickle stream has no identity in the larger stream because it is overwhelmed, just like your psyche may be lost in the energy signatures of a visiting extraterrestrial. If the ego is overwhelmed, it may believe you are dying or have died, which is really bad news for any future plans you may have, as it may return to the spirit and never come back.

Even if you can handle the energies and keep your ego and wits about you, the entity Zariyah advises attempting any such contact before one is prepared is to risk psychic shock. In order to achieve an energetic "middle ground" for contact, the energy frequencies between the parties WILL involuntarily equalize and merge once they come into contact with each other. Anything that keeps your vibrational frequency range below that middle ground will be released, which sounds good, but in effect is just the opposite. When that happens, all of your trauma energy and beliefs, which you have not released, all of your unresolved fears, traumas, angers, victimhoods, and/or any other negative attachment you have energetically stored in your being will flood your consciousness in one intense moment with an immediacy and presence your mental faculties will be unable to handle.

Those same issues and hurts you have not processed and released will flood your mind at once. If you haven't resolved each of them since they happened, how will you handle resolving all of them in an instant? It will be the worst horror story you have ever conceived, and it has no happy ending. Your mental processes may "short-circuit," resulting in psychic shock. Fears are a huge obstacle for some preparing for Open Contact; for this reason, fears of abandonment or death are the most prominent because they hold such a powerful grip on our psyche. Suddenly having them activated in their full emotional impact will literally be too much for our minds to bear. And if you believed it possible you were dying at the time of contact, or you were going to die when you faced an alien, the results may be catastrophic, as the ego may leave the body and never return. Another example would be to think of your brain as a single LED bulb that requires very little electricity to be activated, and then suddenly being powered by the 220 volts it takes to run a house furnace or air conditioner. If the voltage sent from the source isn't effectively dampened before sending, or by a "resistor" of some sort to stop the extra voltage from reaching the LED bulb, or the bulb's ability to accept the greater voltage is not increased, your brain will fry or short out and cease to function. That being said, personal contact is not for the faint of heart. Prepare well and give yourself the chance to experience the excitement and magic of your personal contact event. Do it before you are ready, and you will never be the same for reasons best not considered, and you will miss all the excitement!

Chapter Eleven

Bringing Contact Closer to You

If you would like to take other actions to help prepare for your own personal contact experience, I have several ideas and a couple of exercises for you. I suggest utilizing the ones that appeal to you, but they are all helpful in establishing intent and taking physical action towards achieving that goal. These are good practices for general manifestation, such as visualizations, but they're tailored to this specific outcome.

The first starts with supportive affirmations repeated three times a day to help ingrain that energy, especially if you feel joy when saying it, which energizes not only the memory but also aids in its manifestation. An example would be: "My personal contact experience will greatly enhance my life," or "I had a great Open Contact event!" Make sure whatever you choose is short, assumes you will have the experience, and reflects the effect it will have on your life.

One way to enhance your ability to experience contact is to create a mental meeting room to welcome the being and make your connection. Your imaginary meeting room will serve as an informational conduit for the alien being who has chosen to communicate with you. By earnestly and imaginatively exploring events around Open Contact, a literal mental construct is created that can enable contact preparation to proceed more effectively. That space is not physical, of course, and enables the two-way exchange of information on conscious and subconscious levels, and aligns your individual vibrational frequency range with the specific extraterrestrial being. This "meeting room" will allow the alien being to help direct your imagination more efficiently, guiding playful mental explorations so you experience Open Contact scenarios in more meaningful ways. This will most likely be the first contact you've had, and the mental meeting room is a great place to be introduced before you see any "off-world" being face-to-face. Remember to feel excited and keep your vibration high. It helps.

Another playful exercise is to pretend all beings you see: humans, animals, insects…are really aliens exploring your planet. Do this in a freeform manner by letting the images flow to you instead of generating them in your mind. Give them their own histories and Earth agendas. Make up a story about the planet or galaxy they are from and why they chose to be on Earth at this time, but be positive about it—no conquest themes please! Think about how they might view our world. What can they observe that humans can't? Really play with it for a minute or two, and remember to ramp up your excitement so you can experience those beings. This exercise can help solidify your contact experience into reality, not only by reinforcing your desire for contact, but by helping your ego to be open to new ideas and experiences, and to know that things are not really what they seem. As you get used to the freeform ideas coming to your mind, you make it easier for images to be presented to you to help guide those mental explorations in more meaningful ways. That is an important outcome of this exercise because it will establish a relationship between you and helpful beings, enabling you to receive their messages more efficiently.

A third mental exercise focuses more on the contact event itself. By meditating on how you believe the Open Contact may actually transpire, you open up more possibilities and avenues for the actual contact event to occur. Again, let your mind play with the idea and flesh out as many details as you can mentally hold until you can feel the event. Make up a story about your contact event. Writing it down is also helpful. An example would be: "You tingle as you know the frequency of the excitement you feel and the preparations you have made are helping attract the being you have seen in your dreams. You tremble a little, allowing yourself a release of pent-up excitement at this day finally happening as the shimmering ship lands before you. You feel your nervousness transform into exhilaration, and your gleeful breath escapes your body to be replaced by a mindful, deep cleansing breath of calm. You know you are prepared for this. You better be, because the ship door just opened and here it comes…" You get the idea. Let this exercise of freeform thought, attraction, and connection be like an in-depth exploration of "what if." Build on each succeeding exercise by adding new details or by allowing the scene to progress further into your contact timeline. Where do you go? What do you do? You have the idea. Now go play with it, and don't forget to feel!

Another valuable tool for preparing for Open Contact is to establish a galactic identity. Literally thinking of yourself and taking physical actions to identify yourself as an intergalactic being open to engaging and connecting with your galactic friends and neighbors, perhaps from constellations you may know.

Bashar recommends making an Interstellar Alliance ID card to carry with you, and gives explicit instructions on how to do so if you need more information. Bashar says taking that step of forming a galactic identity is a key component to moving you closer to your Open Contact event. That identity is Step Four of The Interstellar Social Experiment, which Bashar introduced in June 2024. Bashar also discusses the Interstellar Alliance, which is a galactic organization humanity will be part of as we progress towards becoming Homo galacticus. You can carry other IDs, of course, but keep your galactic ID with you as a reminder of who you are, and make it part of your new identity. Become a resident and representative of Earth, eager to meet and learn from your new friends. You are part of something larger than humanity itself. You can incorporate your new identity into your exercises, also. Maybe use it to order drinks at your own *Star Wars* bar scene, perhaps. A bit of mental play to help you have a face-to-face meeting with a being from another world? Sounds like a fun way to build excitement.

If you can do it, dream work can be another valuable tool for manifesting. First, for beginners, please understand that each person having an Earthly experience also has a "dreaming self," which is a necessary functional counterpart to our waking identity. Only the dreaming self has freedom from the physical reality "rules" of time, space, and matter, and operates in a perfect environment to help establish the vibration necessary for your personal contact to occur. While it may sound a bit far-fetched to some, actively working towards Open Contact in the dream state is a natural fit for both humans and extraterrestrials, and the most likely venue for initial contact. For humans, it would be easier to accept contact while in the dream state because it would not directly affect the psyche or bodily conditions. The contacting being would also not have to reduce their vibration to the point necessary to physically appear in our physical world to coach us, but could still engage in meaningful interactions to make contact more furtive. It also allows for a natural telempathic connection, helping not only to prepare us for the actual contact event, but may also help in retaining and relaying information and direction to your conscious, waking self. The dream environment also gives the extraterrestrials an idea of your personality and where you are in the process to help them determine the optimum path for contact, and helps them screen or evaluate us free-will humans, which have been known to be unpredictable at times. Just a precaution for them. Like not picking up hitchhikers around prisons.

If you can lucid dream, even better, as you can consciously interact with your alien dream host to greatly speed up the contact preparations. If you are not familiar with lucid dreaming, it may behoove you to learn how, or at least learn more about it. Robert Waggoner is a well-known expert in the field. Even if you do not normally remember your dreams, you can still set the intention before sleep that you will work on preparing your mind and body for your personal contact event during sleep. Orienting your head to the north will also help you remember your dreams. Whether you actively participate in your contact dream work or not, know and believe it is helping you and moving you closer to your own personal contact event. You may find yourself not only enabling and experiencing contact in the dream state, but perhaps even in group dreams with hundreds or more individuals participating in a mass dream experience prior to the actual global Open Contact event in 2027. We will have a much more active dream life after Open Contact, as our higher vibration will allow us to coordinate and work in groups to a large degree.

The last preparation suggestion is to educate yourself on as many aspects of the coming contact events as possible. Focus on the event as if you were a detective gathering details like *the four Ws and how*. Information to answer all of those questions is already available if you know the proper sources. I have mentioned several already, which provide valid information and specific details. They and others can be found on the internet. There are a multitude of books, videos, and programs on the most popular streaming sites and social media. You can even search for a local channeler, as there are more than a million channelers bringing forth channeled beings in most likely a hundred different languages. There is a growing wave of devotees to alien contact, and more entities desiring to come in and speak through a human than there are humans able and willing to host. They are not only interested in ushering in the contact event, but in raising the vibration of the Earth Collective to enable an exciting new chapter in the evolution of humanity and every Earth species. As Zariah said, "It's the best party in town."

As a review, I will let Bashar close out this piece as he has a very concise way of getting his messages across in his own direct and personable way. In his video *Countdown to Contact Year One (2024)*,

Bashar describes the important characteristics that nourish Open Contact:

"Love, peace, creativity, imagination, and

a willingness to be your true selves,

a willingness to raise your vibration,

a willingness to expand your consciousness,

a willingness to connect to All-That-Is in a variety of ways."

Bashar expands on that message by adding, "the idea is to know: within yourself, within your mind, within your soul, within your heart, that you are not alone. And to open up your hearts and your minds and your spirits to the understanding that you are connected to the cosmos, that you are part of a galactic family and a spiritual family, that you are not alone, that has to be real to you."

I couldn't have said it better myself.

If you wish to explore more of what our world will be like after Open Contact, the Future Pleiadians have provided a Public Service Announcement to address the coming changes. A glimpse of our future you might say. You can find that session here:

https://youtu.be/jALTTcIaPCI

Thank you for dedicating your time to learning more about your future and humanity's future as well. If you choose to prepare yourself for open contact, you will find many things happen. As your vibration rises, the people you no longer resonate with will fade away, and you will lose them. You will feel lost at times, unsure of your role and/or what you should do. That is not a true loss, but a realignment and reset of who you are. And new people who do resonate with you will show up, and so will those who have the information you need to grow. You will feel the need to create because when you create, you are opening yourself up to creative energy, and it is easier for other beings to guide you and add their energy to your experience. You will also be triggered. All triggers are gifts, as they are messages you still hold those energies and beliefs within you which no longer serve you, as discussed in this book. That is where the End-of-Life Review can be a great asset to your spiritual journey. And you can do this. The proof is you are right here, right now, reading this book. I have faith in you, and I have been there. I guarantee you it is a rewarding path, but not without challenges, as they never end. It is how we grow. May you grow into your knowing, and may you love yourself enough to welcome change and to push through uncomfortable stages to forge the new you you choose to be. And I will meet you there, on the other side of Open Contact. May the love of the Hybrid Children be with you and guide you wherever you are.

Ray Heitman

Postscript from the Hybrid Children

"And we have come to celebrate our book. And we are celebrating because we wish for you to know it is not just our book. It is not just humanity's book. This is a book for all of the interested beings who are observing and participating in Open Contact. That is the focus. The focus is Open Contact that requires building awareness, and then building acceptance. And then, once that happens, then things can proceed in a more tangible fashion for you. Not that you can't feel the energies already, but when you see the various beings who get to come in, the Pleiadians and the Yahyels, and then us. We're not sure exactly, well, we're not in the… in those meetings, per se, about how humans get introduced to us lovely Hybrid Children yet. But it may just be pictures, or it may just be some kind of press conference where they let everybody know that we will be coming in. So that part has to be worked out. We have time, we have time. We have your time as well.

But we wish for everybody to understand that this book is merely a stepping stone. It is part of a process. And you guys are all involved in this process. Because you may think that you are waiting for Open Contact, but that is not the case. You are actually participating in Open Contact at this very moment. Because it is not a flip of the switch. It is a melding. It is a building. It is a cascading eruption of information, and it will flood into your social structures, your governmental and environmental, and educational and financial systems. It will affect them all when it comes flooding in to them, and they will not be able to withstand the new energy which is coming in, which will lift everyone up. And we do mean everyone. Now, it will not be at the same time. It will not be at the same time. But there will be enough, because unless there's enough, then it's not gonna happen. It's that tipping point. And that is something in metaphysical circles which gets batted around. But it is kind of a loose thing. People don't understand exactly what it is, but it's more of the vibrational levels for the required number of individuals. So that humans can tolerate our energies. They can acclimate themselves to what we have to offer on an energetic basis. They can lift, or they can accept being lifted up in those ways for those amount of time that we will be before them. And not only us, but the Pleiadians and the Yahyel's, our Teachers."

Hybrid Children channeled by Ray Heitman 3/29/26 (No video)

Questioner: Is there anything that we can do to help prepare our family and friends that may not be as knowledgeable as this group might be?

"You can play with them. You can start games. But the most important thing is to just love them. Love them unconditionally. Because that raises their vibration when they feel that, when they feel that closeness, when they can physically touch that energy, because it warms them inside. And raising that vibration, we've always talked about, oh, it ripples out, ripples out, ripples out. Because it does! And they will be lifting up every person who they come into contact with, provided they're not super crabby, we will say. But as far as information, they still have to be ready. But the book and the other movies that are coming out, because this is a well-choreographed event. It is all coming. It is a "now showing" or "coming soon!

"These are all (movie) trailers for Open Contact. And once those start coming in faster and faster and faster, and the ship sightings start happening more often and for longer periods and over more populated areas, then there will be no denying that all of this is happening. And then people will want answers. They will say, what do you think about that? Or that kind of stuff. They'll be bombarding social media, and the news organizations saying, "Hey, I want to know more, I want to know more!" And when you hear your friends and family asking

184

about that kind of stuff, then you can politely say to them, well, I can tell you what I understand. Or you could just give them our book. Do both!"

Hybrid Children channeled by Ray Heitman 3/29/26 (No video)

Glossary

This glossary is organized into loose categories of terms, hybrid types, and channelers, in that order. Please understand that the definitions below are not meant to replace dictionary definitions; they are my personal definitions based on what I recall and the knowledge I may have acquired. As such, this information should not be assumed to be complete, let alone completely accurate. I welcome knowledgeable corrections.

In fact, these definitions are meant to rise above dictionary definitions by adding not only my personal experience and insight to them, but also to get you to think about your own personal definitions, as well as acquaint you with words, phrases, and concepts you may not be familiar with. They will come in handy in our future, and I hope they are informative and entertaining, as my Leo ego loves appreciation.

At your service,

Ray Heitman

Glossary Terms

Andromedan – A nonphysical race from the Andromeda Galaxy, who are very loving and knowledgeable, but do not care for any rules or restrictions. They appear to be rather brusque and mock humans at times, but mostly because it makes them likable. They do have a sense of humor and a strong sense of duty to themselves and doing what they desire. One of the four main space races involved in helping humans evolve into Homo galacticus.

Anunnaki (or Anu) – An ancient spacefaring race that, in ways, broke contact protocols by genetically altering existing Earth hominids like Homo habilis and Homo erectus and infusing them with portions of their DNA so they would be suited to mining certain minerals they needed to save their planetary environment. The Anu were discovered and sent back to their planet, but by then, humans had been created, and the world of extraterrestrials has been babysitting us ever since. The Anunnaki evolved into the Lyrans and some Pleiadian races.

Astral Realm – A reference to the region of consciousness related to the Akashic Records, which contain a wee bit of consciousness and worldview of every life that has existed within the Earth realm. It is akin to a living record of those lives and will be accessible to almost all humans within ten years after Open Contact.

Auric Field – The energetic field given off by all humans to indicate their emotional state and other energies, which is commonly seen as a color gradient with each color signifying a certain emotional energy.

Baneesha – A Yahyel hybrid who is one of the Hybrid Children's Teachers who agreed to do a channeling session with me in order to provide more information for their book, and did an excellent session.

Channeling – A communication method where a consciousness "speaks" through another being using the being's vocabulary and voice. The messages received must be translated into language, and all such communications will have some distortion based on the capabilities, beliefs, and biases of the channeler.

Christ Consciousness – The energy of the divine consciousness interpreted as "Christ" by the Western world religions, which is actually a cyclical loving energy that returns to our earth plane approximately every 2,000 years. It is exemplified by the unconditional love of the Hybrid Children.

Counterpart – A being related to another conscious exploration by a soul. Many believe it is any being in the same soul "group," which is true, but counterparts can extend beyond a soul group as well. I have been in contact with several of mine personally, including one among the Future Pleiadian group I channel and another from an artificial

188

water world planet beyond the star Cygnus called Ess, which is populated by the Ess-Kadaya.

CPS – Cycles per second.

Earth Collective – The total combined consciousness and energies of the Earth and all consciousness in or upon it.

Enclave – The name given by Bashar for the groupings of Hybrid Children on Earth for acclimation to our climate and other reasons before they come to live and teach among us.

Extraterrestrial – A designation made by humans for physical entities that are nonhuman. There are an unknown number of them, but it is most likely millions.

Future Pleiadians – A nonphysical group of Pleiadians from the seventh density and 400 years into our linear future on another timeline, which first connected with me in Feb of 2025. I named them Future Pleiadians as they are in my "future," and they have been and continue to be instrumental in my channeling growth, as they created and maintain the communication conduit that over one hundred different beings have used to come forth during my personal channeling sessions. A female counterpart of mine is part of this group, which is why I was chosen for my various roles related to them and why they worked so diligently to connect with me. I can try to teach you how to call them in in channeling if you reach out to me, or you can go to their YouTube channel and search for channeling, or click here – https://www.youtube.com/watch?v=cvzFrFZEZk0&t=7s

You can find out more about them by viewing the early March 2025 sessions. I confess I have been recruited to help them obtain more perspectives of Open Contact, which is one of the reasons they chose to connect with me. Many in our High Vibe Channeling group are assisting them, and in my understanding, they use me as a reward and dangle my channeling ability to many beings who enjoy novel experiences like never having experienced being a physical human, or for some, never having experienced any type of physical consciousness expression at all, in exchange for their perspectives on Open Contact.

The Great Reset – In my understanding, it is the name coined by extraterrestrials for the period between when Open Contact occurs and when humans begin to evolve into Homo galacticus around the year 2050. It also represents the beginning of humans becoming a space-faring race, openly welcoming extraterrestrial races who live with us and visit us on Earth, and the great prosperity and achievement of the human race.

Greys – A civilization which became expert geneticists and created the hybrid race of beings of which the Hybrid Children are part, as well as the other hybrid races which will be part of humanity's future. The Greys chose technology and mental improvements over emotional importance and ended up losing the ability not only to feel but also to reproduce. They discovered how to travel through time-space coordinates and tried to keep their lineage alive by creating hybrid beings by mixing human DNA with their own. Unfortunately, lacking emotions, they did not understand that taking humans aboard their spaceships could be traumatic for those participating. Even though the higher selves of the humans agreed with the procedures, the humans were unaware, and this was the basis for the abduction stories. The original race of Greys is not extinct.

Homo Galacticus – The next evolutionary form of humanity, which encompasses abilities and physical senses beyond humans born before approximately the year 1990, like telempathy, a higher vibrational resonance, and more expansive DNA structures.

Hybrid – A mixed DNA being of human and extraterrestrial genetic stock, which was engineered by the Greys to help them continue their legacy and to keep their lineage alive after they rendered themselves no longer able to reproduce or feel emotions after excessive tinkering with their DNA.

Hybrid Children – A race of the most delightful and unconditional loving beings who lead with the heart and desire the best for all living things, which is a mission they are well-prepared for. They are a box of giggles, a warm hug from a best friend, and the teachers and bridge for our new evolution of humanity and planetary conscious unity.

Hybrid Parent – The misnamed phrase coined for humans to represent a hybrid being's biological link to a human whose DNA was utilized in the creation of a hybrid being.

Lyrans – Loving beings from the star system Lyra, which can have feline characteristics if they choose to be physical. They love and hold dear all life forms and are very advanced and interested in assisting developing civilizations, like Earth. They are as peaceful and loving as they come.

Mediumship – A person who utilizes a connection to the astral realm to relay information to others.

Open Contact – The name given to the coming global public announcement that humans and governments have been in contact with extraterrestrial races for decades, which culminates with the introduction of the Yahel and Pleiadian races. This term is actually a result of the phasing in of awareness.

Pleiadians – A generic term for the many societies and beings of the Pleiades star system. They are very loving and supportive of other races and seem to be more "hands-on" than other representatives of our galactic family. When they choose a physical representation, they closely resemble humans, which is not only representative of their influence in our creation but also why they will be among the first two extraterrestrial races introduced to humans, along with the Yahyel.

Portals – Access points or doorways used by various energies and entities to move between dimensions and/or locations. There is a wide variety of them, and the auric field of humans can be used as a portal for certain individuals in certain cases.

Sasquatch – A loving, interdimensional being who evolved from natural Earth hominids who were not "tampered" with by the Anunnaki. They have ancient and incredible wisdom and identify strongly with the energies and consciousness of all Earth creatures and Mother Earth herself. They can alter their vibration so they are no longer visible to humans, which gives them the "slip-walker" moniker. They are naturally playful and caring and will be interacting with humans as part of the Great Reset. All of my personal experiences with them have been fantastic, and they frequently overwhelm me with love when I think about them.

Spirit Realm – The level above physicality, which is signified by a vibrational frequency range of greater than 333,000 cps.

Tall Whites – The third group of beings I channeled are multidimensional beings, which are masters of maintaining and controlling energies so that other beings can experience realities in a seamless fashion. They have chosen me to be a spokesperson for them when the time comes, and contacted me initially to help learn about humans and to build awareness of them on their terms, as their energy will be detectable by humans once they achieve a higher vibration after Open Contact.

Teachers – The general name given by the Hybrid Children for those loving and capable beings dedicated to nurturing and educating them for their various missions. The Teachers predominately belong to the Yahyel race, but other races, including humans, fall under that category.

Telempathy – The ability to send and receive complex information and emotions to and from others by thought.

Telepathy – The ability to send and receive information through a language to and from others by thought.

Timeline – A reference to other lives humans lead, parallel or otherwise, that we live out as "other" lives related to our Earthly incarnation. Timelines are also related to "probable selves," which take the paths not chosen by our decisions in our Earthly lives, branch off, and live out that reality unbeknownst to us from our physical existence. That reality is just as valid as the life we experience.

Watchers – The general name given by the Hybrid Children for anyone who connects with them who is not a Hybrid Child or a Teacher.

The Hybrid Races

Maz'eh – The first hybrid race created by the Greys to preserve their lineage.

Maz'ani – The second hybrid race created by the Greys, which is more human-like.

Sassani – The third hybrid race, which is quasi-physical and involved as the point race for the coordination of the Open Contact scenarios. They have silky skin, draw most of their energy from their environment, and are telepathically connected to all of their race. Several prominent channeled Sassani beings are Bashar, Ryokah, and Elan.

Sha'ya'el – The fourth hybrid race the Greys created, which are very loving and are teachers and guides to the Yahyel race.

Ya'ya'el or Yahyel – The fifth hybrid race of beings created by the Greys, and the hybrid race most resembling humans, enough so that they may walk among us now without attracting undue attention. The loving Teachers of the Hybrid Children, along with many other roles related to their explorations and Open Contact. They will be one of the two extraterrestrial races to meet humans publicly as part of Open Contact, along with the Pleiadians.

Sha'linya or Shalanaya – The Sassani name for the Hybrid Children, which means First Ones in their ancient language. They are the bridge to humanity's future by integrating with humans and blending with them to create the next evolution of humanity: the Enanika.

E'nanni'ka or Enannika – The next evolution of humanity after the new generations born during the last two decades and ongoing blend with the Hybrid Children to produce a new species of humans, called Homo galacticus. The majority of them will be able to communicate with the spirit realm and have telempathy.

Anu'Het or Anu Het – The further and final evolution of humanity. The Anu'Het are a combination of humans and all of the other hybrid races, and will become nonphysical beings, but not for another one thousand or so years after Open Contact.

<u>**Channelers and their related groups or entities**</u>

Aisling O'Donnell – The well-traveled and gifted channeler of Zariyah from Orion. She is the author of *Arcana*, has been channeling for several years, and holds a doctorate in philosophy.

Zariyah - A seventh-dimensional consciousness and counterpart of Aisling O'Donnell, who is an excellent source of relevant and deep understanding and information. You can find videos of Zariyah on the YouTube channel Dark Star Channeling.

Leslie Stewart – An author, wonderfully nice person, and channeler of the group of beings she named Orion.

Orion – A star system that had thousands and thousands of years of inner conflict and authoritarian regimes that even monitored individual thoughts in some ways. With the help of an enlightened child and later a priest, they realized their reality was an illusion, and that if they stopped providing energy to something, it ceased to have an impact on their lives. They achieved their ascension into a nonphysical race without the help of any other space-faring race. It is the home star system of Zariah, channeled by Aisling O'Donnell. This name is also the name of a collective consciousness group channeled by Leslie Stewart.

Heidi Slater – An intuitive energy worker and talented channeler of the Divine Love Collective who works with children with learning disabilities in her 3D life.

Divine Love Collective – A group of very loving celestial and angelic entities, and more channeled by Heidi Slater.

Isabelle Rohach Zimmerman – An experienced author, channeler, and teacher of other teachers and healers, Isabelle is a delight to behold and enjoy. She connects to Isis, Athena, angels, and other divine beings who make up her Divine Crystaline Collective. You can find her books here:

The Mighty Tiny Awakening Handbook https://a.co/d/9AKjRfr

Unseen Light (The Light: The Fae Union Trilogy)
https://a.co/d/dELIfwI

Divine Crystalline Collective – A very loving and energetic group of angelic beings and other divine energies, including the Hybrid Children, Isis, Athena, and more.

Darryl Anka – A profound and creative author, metaphysical teacher and conference headliner, and the channeler of Bashar for over 40 years. He is one of, if not the leading provider of channeled messages for the English-speaking population and has millions of followers and devotees. I follow him regularly.

Bashar – A well-known channeled being for over 40 years with millions of followers worldwide, channeled by Darryl Anka. They sell out large venues and have books and BasharTV, as well as presences on most social media outlets. Bashar is a "go-to" for valuable and relevant information about our galactic family, Earth history and secrets, and Open Contact.

Tyler Ellison – A certified instructor of the Universal Healing Dao, metaphysical magician, acupuncturist, and excellent channeler of Ryokah and Egyptian gods, archangels, and other divine beings, is also an author and alchemist, and a big draw at related conferences.

Tyler offers a wide variety of valuable services, which can be found on his website thegalacticguide.com. I enjoy all of his material and find it exceptional.

Ryokah – A Sassani being and The Galactic Guide channeled by Tyler Ellison, who provides very detailed insights and wisdom about a seemingly endless array of subjects, is a great source of information relevant to our current day and our future. Ryokah frequently provides lessons and instruction for making changes to our lives and holds weekly channeling sessions on YouTube and is a featured channeler at many large events. One of my favorite entities!

Dante "Starshine" Filipini – An author, healer, spiritual counselor, world traveler, and a deep channeler of The Pleiadian Council. Visit his YouTube channel and his website heartflowtransmissions.com, where you can find his books, book private sessions, and learn more about this very interesting individual and his passions.

The Pleiadian Council – A spiritual group of many different extraterrestrial races and energies channeled by Dante "Starshine" Filipini, which provides deep insights and relevant information to help us become better versions of ourselves and enlighten us with information about subjects that are of interest to us.

Ray Heitman – A quick-witted and humorous human who claims to have "more fun than humanly possible" due to the frequency of participation of various nonhuman entities in all of his waking and sleeping moments. After decades of writing, he was told to write this book, and a couple of others, and he will be writing more until he is told to stop. He also founded High Vibe Channeling and has channeled over one hundred beings during his sessions. He is keeper of the local forest, is addicted to flowers, bowls well with either hand, and shares his home with his beloved pit-mix Ollie Charisma, who has a growing following on Facebook.

Channeling Beings of Light – The name of the first YouTube channel and entities to be channeled by Ray Heitman. They are a very loving, nonphysical group which specializes in bending and blending light forms, and the source of Ray's Earthly consciousness explorations. https://www.youtube.com/@ChannelingBeingsofLight

Channeling Future Pleiadians & Friends – The second YouTube channel of Ray Heitman featuring the Future Pleiadians, but also including the Hybrid Children, Sasquatch, Andromedans, Tall Whites, Inner Earth Beings, and more.
https://www.youtube.com/@ChannelingFuturePleiadians

Channeling Hybrid Children – The third YouTube channel for Ray Heitman and the name of one of his Facebook pages, both exclusively featuring the Hybrid Children group channeled by Ray.
https://www.youtube.com/@ChannelingHybridChildren

High Vibe Channeling – The name of a Facebook Page, YouTube channel, and the channeling group founded in 2024 and managed by Ray Heitman. The group has multiple channeling sessions each week from a variety of gifted channelers. The YouTube page is also used to post some of Ray Heitman's personal channeling, like the Open Invitation ET Contact sessions. The YouTube link is here:
https://www.youtube.com/@HighVibeChanneling

Usol – A group of nonphysical beings involved in humanity's linear future and the funniest beings I have ever channeled. They have even told jokes in sessions before and admitted their name is a play on words and a bad pronunciation of "us all." They thrive on interactions with attendees and have a deep sensing and connection with those who experience their energy. Their sessions can be found by searching for them on the High Vibe Channeling YouTube page. They told me I am an aspect of them, meaning a creation of their group of consciousness, whatever that means. They also show up and protect me from unexpected occurrences during the Open Invitation ET Contact sessions, such as when one who learned by consuming naturally tried to consume my consciousness, and others had to be removed if they did not play nice or their energy was not a good fit for me. Their channeling sessions can be found on High Vibe Channeling and Channeling Future Pleiadians YouTube channels.

Open Invitation ET Contact – The name given to the channeling sessions allowed by the Future Pleiadians, where they allow or funnel a parade of different beings through the communication conduit they have established for their communication. It is possible that the Future Pleiadians trade this unique opportunity to experience humanity or physicality in exchange for accessing the entity's views on Open Contact, which is a strong desire of the Future Pleiadians. The Usol generally watch over these sessions and control which ones come through. Over one hundred different beings have come through these sessions, from insectoids, arachnids, nonphysical beings, symbiotic beings, and many that have never experienced physical life of any kind. These sessions are available on the High Vibe Channeling YouTube channel.

Glossary Terms – Per the Hybrid Children

Note – I thought it would be interesting to include the glossary terms for the Hybrid Children, and I was correct. They are so much fun! Read below to find more of their wisdom and humor for yourself. With thanks to Leslie Stewart for helping me conduct this session. The video link for this session is at the bottom of their glossary.

<u>Glossary Session with Leslie Stewart</u>

Hybrid Children: We are here, and you guys are funny. You guys are funny. You make fun of other people in a nice, non-malicious way. It is just a way of humoring each other and in raising your vibrations. And more power to you for that! There is no laughter that got hurt in this exchange. And that is one way of looking at it, because laughter only builds things up for the most part, unless your ego gets involved. And we understand that this is for a session, for the lesson, for the book, for us, for awareness, for the worrrrrld! So, and we thank you, we thank you, thank you for your part in this exercise that we will say.

1:04 into the video

Leslie: My pleasure.

Hybrid Children: And without further ado do, we can let you go and give us the terms, and we will give you the words.

Leslie: All right. Hybrid Children.

Hybrid Children: Yayyyy! Where? Where? Where? Oh! We know where! We're connected. That is, that is a, a bunch of loving individuals who practice unconditional love as a birthright. They are a connective species, a bridge to many, many, many different loving races of beings, of expressions of consciousness. And they will unite many different aspects and portions and segments of the galactic families together, and bring in a unity to the Earth, or help bring in unity to the Earth of your entire consciousness. Although that will take some time to settle in, it will simmer for quite a while before it is ready to be consuuuumed by the galactic universe.

Leslie: Yes.

Hybrid Children: And we love them like we love everybody else.

Leslie: The Future Pleiadians.

2:22 into the video

Hybrid Children: Oh, they are so helpful! They are helpful. Yes, they are our friennnnnds! They are everybody's friends who knows them. They are literally without enemies! Because they are so loving and they are so helpful and so expressive and they really, really lay out the welcome mat for *everybody*. And with their powers and their perspectives and their wah, massive amounts of wisdom, they can orchestrate some really neat happenings amongst all of the physical and a lot of the non-physical beings. Because they just know how to treat people and how to lead them and how to love them in the best way that they know how. And it's, it's for their own purposes, because that is how they expand as well. But they are truly friends for all! And we love them. Like we love everybody. Woohoo. There's a theme.

3:24 into the video

Leslie: High Vibe Channeling.

Hybrid Children: Oh, that's, that's the group! That's the group! That's the group! We've been there. We've been there. We got the t-shirt. Um, um, um, it is, it is a group of individuals who have come together, uh, who have generally like minds, who have open hearts and are looking for different ways or avenues of expressions of not only learning and growing and expanding on their own, but for other individuals who they can connect with, and build relationships with. And to share that knowledge, to share their perspectives. And to grow closer as part of an Open Contact scenario. Because each of the members and attendees of that group will have specific roles when Open Contact comes. Mostly in their own generic areas or communities we will say. But there will be some which do expand a bit and maybe perhaps travel to help relay the story and awareness and build um, um, favorable attrib, or attitudes towards those extraterrestrials and towards us and towards us. Not that we really need the help, but we will take all the help we can get. It's just another expression of lovvve. Woo-hoo! Woo-hoo! Go High Vibe! Go High Vibe!

4:49 into the video

Leslie: Channeling.

Hybrid Children: Oh, we've heard of it. We've heard of it. It is a method of expression of the higher realms, and of other beings who can access the thought patterns and communicate through other beings, and not just necessarily humans. But we can also channel with a lot of the um, larger mammals and that sort of thing to ex, to assess how their readiness is going and what they may need for their fulfillment, and their value fulfillment. And to make sure that they are prepared for the changes that are going to come. But with humans, it's different. Because they are indeed tools of communication for others. They are links in the chain of building awareness. So that is one of the aspects which is utilized along with the dream state connections to help spread knowledge and to help uplift individuals. And to in, in ways which is a minor thing, but it has major effects to anchor some more of that love vibrational energy into your 3D collective realm, because that helps raise the vibration of everyone. Everyone! All consciousness. All consciousness. Woohoo. We're going up, up, up. Yay. So, yeah, that's, that's our answer, and we're sticking to it.

6:13

Leslie: Mediumship.

Hybrid Children: Oh, that's, that's" average ship." But no, that that is more for the astral realm um, fields of information. People who want to talk with those who have died and moved on, who are no longer in the physical. Although they still are in a physical, but you can't perceive them in that physical. But it's still there, trust us. And they can tap into certain energies, the authentic ones can. And they can get information and pass it back and forth. But they generally just stick to that. They have most of them or a lot of them, a significant portion, have limitations that they believe that that is the end of their "powers" we will say. That they can tap into those who are crossing over or who have crossed over, but they may be opening themselves up to extraterrestrial connections as well. Because they are really close. But it is a belief thing which creates some barriers for them to keep them more centered on the Earth-based realities, and personalities, and focuses, and consciousness expressions. Ta-dah!

7:31 into the video

Leslie: Vibrational frequency.

Hybrid Children: Vibrate. Vibe up. Vibe up. Vibe up. Woohoo! Um, yes, that is that is a metric that is used by the extraterrestrial races to help gauge readiness. It is like a temperature gauge for your cooking efforts. Because once things reach the proper temperature, then you know that they are ready to consume. And that's what, that's what, kind of what that is. And we're not going to go into the details on that, but you can read about it in the book and get an idea. That's not exact either, but it's close enough for your world.

8:11 into the video

Leslie: Range. (This was the last word of the previous glossary term, and not a separate term.)

Hybrid Children: Can you speak up? We missed that.

Leslie: Range.

Hybrid Children: Range?

Leslie: Range.

Hybrid Children: We don't understand.

Leslie: I don't either. That's what's on my list. What kind of a range?

Hybrid Children: Well, let's move to the next one.

8:34 into the video

Leslie: Auric field.

Hybrid Children: Auric field. Those are the energetic representations of your emotional states and your thought patterns, which are all combined into, well, they are separate gener, energetic fields, but they are kind of connected in the way that you emanate them. So, they are kind of like overlays of colors. And when you have pure thought and when you have pure happy emotions—all love all the time, then in your expression, those are higher vibrations and lighter colors is the way that humans interpret them. Or have interpreted them, or assigned those particular symbols to them. But it helps. It helps a little bit.

9:26 into the video

Leslie: Homo galacticus.

Hybrid Children: Oh, future humans! Future humans! Yes, those are going to be some of our offspring. Yes, we will meld with the human race and they and then we will have all the cutest babies that you will ever see! Ever experience! It will be wonderful. And they will be telepathic and they can tell you when they need a bottle and they need a change. There's no need to ask them. It'll cut, it'll cut a lot of communication short. There won't be any of that stuff is, "Oh, what's wrong with you, little child?" You will know! And the child will say, "You know dang well what's wrong with me. I already told you!"

Leslie: The Sassani.

Hybrid Children: Oh, yay. Big helpers. Big helpers. Yes. Coordinators. They are the point men. They are, they are helping to control. The traffic cops of Open Contact and beyond, too. And beyond, too. They have this list of protocols which have been decided upon and agreed upon by all of the races which are involved in this particular earth plane scenario, and they are just minding the shop to make sure that everything goes as planned. the

10:42 into the video

Leslie: The Baneesha.

Hybrid Children: Oooo! Teacher, Teacher, Teacher! That is not her name. But we know that is the name that was given to uh, Uncle Ray and, and Mr. Luis too. When they did the session. When they did the session. It's another example of one of the loving teachers and the loving beings which are nurturing us and making sure we get everything that we need. And we mean *everything* that we need! For they are not holding back on any information or anything which might be of service to us. They really are focused on us primarily in ways even more than themselves. And that is a name which was chosen for that particular channeling session and the book, our book. Our book! Woohoo!

11:35 into the video

Leslie: Andromedan

Hybrid Children: Oh, powerhouuuuse. Powerhouuuuse. Yes, they are. They are so loving, and they, they are wonderful to get to know because if they get, if you get to know them, that, that means that they desire to get to know you! Because they're not going to do anything that they don't want to do. For instance, if they were driving a car in your in your um, highways on your Earth and they were going too fast and they got pulled over (by traffic police), the, the they're just going to say, "I don't want to pull over." And they're just going to keep going, and it might cause chaos, and they might just decide (laugh) to discorporate when they do finally decide to stop, but it'll be on their terms. And if you make them stop then they'll find other ways of expressions which suit them, because that's what they like to do. They are, they are a fine example of following your highest vibrations and your desires.

12:38 into the video

Leslie: Pleiadians.

Hybrid Children: Oh. Oh, those are so, there are many, many, many different types of Pleiadians. They might say it's the seven sisters, but there's brothers in there, too. And they look a lot like you. They look a lot like you. And that's on purpose. And that is one of the reasons why you look the way you do. Because this was planned and they knew, and others knew, other beings, other races, that eventually, once you had evolved enough, that you would be open to extraterrestrial connections. But there had to be beings like you to help you make that jump. Make that leap into your next evolution. So they were, you were chosen to look a lot like them. And with the Yahyels, it was different because they have a little bit more of your DNA for their aesthetic qualities, we will say. But with the Pleiadians, they had input in that, and they said, "Yeah, make them look like us, and we'll come down, and we'll help them." We'll, we'll shepherd this one into their new reality.

13:47 into the video

Leslie: Lyran

Hybrid Children: Louder, please.

Leslie: Lyrans.

Hybrid Children: Oh. Oh, the, the kitties, the feline. Yes. Very loving. Very loving. And they care about, they care deeply about every living thing. And they want to protect them all. And they do if they can. And they will not ever fight or have uh, conflicts or anything like that because they've been around for a long, long, long, long time. And they have learned not only to protect themselves by avoiding such situations, but also by manipulating energy so they do not have to come into contact with those types of things. But yes, and if you pet them, they purr. They might only do it just to please you, but that will work.

14:39 into the video

Leslie: Open Contact

Hybrid Children: Oh, Party! Party! It's, it's, it's a long series of events which culminate in the introduction of the Yahyels and the Pleiadians to your kind on a more public basis we will say. There will be governments involved, and some big businesses will be involved. But it will be a shockwave of realization for many on your planet. But that is one of the things that will not happen until your humanity, the Earth Collective, both of them obviously, um, will be ready for it because that shock wave is not meant to knock people down or make them psychotic! It is meant to bring awareness to them and that is what that will do.

15:31 into the video

Leslie: The Great Reset.

Hybrid Children: Ooooo! Ooooo! Party, number two! That's a long time. And well, it's a long party. It's going on forever and ever and ever. Because once you guys make that change, once you get to that level where you are freely interacting with extraterrestrials on your planet and you have accepted your role as space-faring individuals and a space-faring race, then that will truly begin a new evolution and history of humanity. Not just a new chapter, but a brand-new book! Because you will be coming into the space travel. You will be interacting with other civilizations, burgeoning civilizations, and helping them get to where they need to be. And other explorations as well. It will really be not just opening new doors for you, but opening new vast areas of explanations where they don't even know what doors are. You can teach them. We'll be there. We'll be there. And our offspring will help lead the way. Bupp bupp badaaah!

Leslie: But you've already mentioned the Earth Collective.

16:53 into the video

Hybrid Children: Yes. That's everybody and everything all the time. It's, it's the it's, it's a, a group of consciousness of loving beings, many of whom have forgot that they are loving beings. But that is changing too. It is changing by the day, by the minute, by the second. Speaking of by the second, woohoo, it must be time for that.

Leslie: Tall Whites.

Hybrid Children: Oh, they're buddies. They're our buddies. Yes! They're helping fix things. They, they make sure that everything is "just so." And that is cool because they, they don't meddle in other things because that's not their way. They really…it's not that they don't love everything, but they love what they do and what they desire more. And they are focused on that, and everything else that happens outside of that can just happen outside of that. And if they need to know, they'll know. But yes, they are, they are good fixers, and they are good um, lovers of not only continuity, but fluidity, and organization, and a complex juggling and intermingling of energies that come with so many different races intermingling with each other. And they have a special fondness for Earth. They really do. Whether they tell you or not.

18:25 into the video

Leslie: Ahh. The Anunnaki.

Hybrid Children: Anunnaki. Wooo! What troublemakers they are, or they were. They have since evolved. Yes. Into the Lyrans and the Pleiadians, as Uncle Ray would say. But yes, they came around, and they were in trouble, and they wanted some helpmates 'cause they're like, "This is too much work for us to do. We'll be dead by the time we get done." So they took some of your primates, and they said, "Oh, look. We're going to inject you with this stuff and make you talk to us, and then we can manage you in a more productive manner and make you like us a little bit." And then, as a mean trick on reality, they actually created religion. Because some of them desired to be worshiped, and they said, "Oh, this is pretty cool." Until everybody else found out about it, and they said, "Oh, banished. Oh, that's not so cool."

19:25 into the video

Leslie: Teachers.

Hybrid Children: What's that?

Leslie: Teachers.

Hybrid Children: Louder, please.

Leslie: Teachers.

Hybrid Children: Teachers!!!

Leslie: Teachers.

Hybrid Children: Ohhh. Oh! Oh! Oh! Those are, those are wonderful! We give our hearts. And they live in our hearts, and they are really magnificent individuals. All of them. And not only just the Yahyels, but they are predominantly Yahyels. There are some others like human teachers like Uncle Ray, like Uncle Ray. And, and others who bring us through like you, like you. And many other people of High Vibe Channeling too. But yes, Teachers are...they're so informative, and they're so knowing and loving and caring. They are like the best stewards of new life forms that we could ever hope to have.

20:14 into the video

Leslie: Watchers.

Hybrid Children: Oooo! We have billions of those because our energies are available to all loving beings. And almost all beings are loving to a great, great extent. And those who wish to learn more about us can just connect with one of us and then they are, not really astounded that they can connect to all of us through one of us, but that requires our participations too in ways. But it is just a loving exchange of information and connection and love energy and knowing and wisdom and acclimating to each other and figuring out what everyone else needs. That is a big soup of personalities and explorations of consciousness which all come together into our awareness. We like that answer.

Leslie: Good answer. Telempathy.

21:16 into the video

Hybrid Children: Oh! You ask us about telempathy and then you want us to put it into words.

Leslie: Mmm- hmm. Hmmm.

Hybrid Children: How ironic! You sure we can't just think it to you?

Leslie: You could.

Hybrid Children: Those it's just thought communications. It's just a wider bandwidth than telepathy is, because telepathy is limited in ways because humans believe that it is speech. It is your language being communicated from one to the other. Mind reading in that way. In that simplified way. But telempathy, it does not have those barriers. It can be everything that you can experience depending on your ability to send and receive it. And your ability for to accept things that are relevant to you too, because some of the stuff, some of the beings they will just not accept some of the trivialities we will say or information which they know that is not in their highest excitement. They will make that part of their Flow so that it kind of bypasses them.

But that is a great tool for your future. And humans will be doing it more and more and more. And you have it you it's awakening now in a very limited way, but you all know about it, and the more people who know about it the more people will say, "Hey I think I'm going to try that." And there are lots of experiments going on around your planet um, by humans and some of those have been planted with impulses we will say, to help get that ball rolling. So we can stir up those thought processes and abilities. And that will be, that will be part of the what you determine the new DNA "awakening" amongst your younger peeps. Amongst those last two generations and those which come on, because they will have that ability already turned on. And it's that's such a foul word for that. They're not "turned on". It's just you tapping into another version of you which already has those abilities. That you have that vibrational match. So you bring that skill set into your awareness of your Now moments.

23:41 into the video

Leslie: Portals.

Hybrid Children: Portals. We're coming through! Those are really like energetic pathways. And (sighs), there are just so many different kinds. And there are some that are just used for specific beings or specific races and some that are more general purpose. And you can view them kind of like wormholes to go from one place to the other. The wormholes on your science fiction, not the ones that are underneath your grass and your weeds and your trees and stuff like that. But, but yes, that is those are (sighs) they're not really doorways. They're not really openings. They're opportunities for stepping through into other portions of vibratory realities.

24:39 into the video

Leslie: Enclave.

Hybrid Children: Ooooo! Home away from home on home! Yes, that, that, that word doesn't mean too much to us, but what it means to us means more to us because that is going to be a grouping of us! And it'll be in specific places around your earth. And not only to protect us, but one of the secrets is, is we will be vibrating at such a high rate that those areas will be lifted up. And in specific locations around the Earth that will form a vibratory grid, which will help energize the Earth as a whole. There is a method to that madness. And we're not be just being kept together because it's good for us and good for you. It's literally good for everybody! Until we get to the point where that acceptance and that awareness is at the proper levels, where we can more freely interact with you and your kind and other animals and beings on your planet as well.

25:53 into the video

Leslie: Sounds exciting. Hybrid parent.

Hybrid Children: Again, please?

Leslie: Hybrid parent.

Hybrid Children: Oh, hybrid parents. Oh, that. That is another term which does not have a lot of meaning for us. Because in reality, everyone is our parent. And that should be apparent to most people. But just because you give a little DNA you think you have some biological claim. But it's not really going to show up in your archeo, archaeological records that way. You can't take a census and list us, oh yeah, well, who's your parents? And we're going to say, well, we have about 300 of them, can we list them all? Because we come from a wide variety of different individuals and races. And all of our attributes are selected specifically for our roles and our missions. And we have just enough human in us to appear as human and to (pause) work those, those emotional tugs to enable humans to love us *very* easily. So that is a term which is good for humans and humans like to use because it gives them some satisfaction, and they feel some sort of connection not only to the word, but it helps them feel like they are part of a hybrid child's life. Or Open Contact in that aspect as well. But for us, it just means an ambiguous circle of love which is related to us. That is our parent. "Love" is our parents.

27:47 into the video

Leslie: Christ consciousness.

Hybrid Children: Again, please?

Leslie: Christ consciousness.

Hybrid Children: Oooooh. Oooooh. Yeah. We've heard of it. It comes around. It comes around. What comes around goes around and it goes around and then it sucks into our heads, and it sucks into our hearts, and then we're like, "Okay, we're loaded up with Christ consciousness. Let's goooo to earth and lift these people up and show them more in a physical way." Not just with speech, but with actions, words, and deeds and vibratory levels. And teach them how unconditional love can come to you and can be practiced and the resulting unity which will come from it. And that is what we are bringing to the planet. We are flying the Christ Consciousness flag! Of course, we fly a lot of flags, even without a flagpole! So, they might be non-physical, but you'll just have to imagine. But yes, that is an energy and a, a love. a distinct and powerful love energy of transformation.

And it comes around every once in a while, like to see if um, it's like the brass ring on the old carousels. To see if you can actually grab a hold of it and take advantage of that love energy to make that break of transformation into a new evolution of heartfelt and heart-led unity. And that's what we are bringing. We're packing our bags full of Christ consciousness and we're going to set up shops on every street corner and we're going to sell it and give away samples.

29:39 into the video

Leslie: All righty. Greys.

Hybrid Children: Greys. Greys. The doctors, expert geneticists. And they said, "Oops, looks like we screwed up and now we can't have any more babies. We better do something about this. I know. Let's take a field trip. We're going to go and sample some DNA and see if we can't make other beings. And maybe we can live on through the histories, through our works, through our hybrids." And they were pioneers in that way. And they created many races. And they created some which were not quite so viable, but those obviously did not continue on. And they, their expertise in that was transferred or learned or integrated by many, many other races and modified as well.

212

And that is how we came into being as well. Because it was all part of the plan. Because when you can dip into the future years in your linear time, and see how things work, then you can move to create other timelines which are more expressive and pref, and allow more opportunities for expansion oppor…and expansions and for explorations in new ways. And that novelty is always going to be at the top of the list for expressions of Source.

Leslie: How about the Sasquatch?

Hybrid Children: Oh, Big buddies. Big buddies. Yes, they're loving. They're in touch with us all the time! They really are because they're love energy and they are watching Earth and they are giving us reports on humans and they really don't need our external help to ascertain where things are going on your world, because they are really in touch with Mother Nature as well. They understand that they are one with the universe and one of the universe and they like to take care of their playgrounds and all creatures upon it. And just by their good wishes, they can increase the vibratory resonance and health of particular beings. They have like magic powers the way humans would interpret it. And they have many, many abilities. And they will be amongst you. It will take some time because you guys, humans have to learn not to be afraid of the big bad wolves which come in many different flavors. Because it's not just the size and the colors and the resonance which matters - it's the heart! And they have big hearts. Their heart is as big as Gaia, as Mother Earth, because that's where they come from.

32:31 into the video

Leslie: How about the Mesa.

Hybrid Children: Maz'eh?

Leslie: Maz'eh. Okay.

Hybrid Children: Yes. Oh, one of the little Greys. Yes. They were, they were the, the, the first introductory efforts to create a human-like race of beings. And while they were loving in ways, they didn't exactly, we don't wish to meet be judgmental, but they did not meet all of the expectations which the Greys had been hoping for. So they decided to try again. And that is the next word on your list.

33:19 into the video

Leslie: Mazani.

Hybrid Children: Ma'zani. And they were tallll grays. And I think that's not really what they were looking for. They, they didn't um, try again because the other ones were too short! They weren't going for a basketball team here, but they were trying to get a race of beings which could help in the Open Contact scenario in ways, and they had their own attributes and their own lives and their own soul paths, we will say. And their own value fulfillments that they were striving for, but it just was not the best fit for the Open Contact scenario. So, as the Greys did, as we are going to tell you to try again! And the Sassani came next. The Sassani came next. They were third. It turned out great. And they're helping. They're returning to Open Contact. Not that they've ever left. But yes, they are really involved in that because they have, they have progressed in a marvelous way in a relatively short amount of time, and non-time, we will say.

34:40 into the video

Leslie: How about the shay, shay Yahyel. Shay ya'el

Hybrid Children: Sha'ya'el?

Leslie: Sha'ya'el. Yes. Oh, thank you.

Hybrid Children: I thought that's what you said. Yes, they came forth. That's, those, those are major teachers for the Yahyels as a matter of fact. Because they are very loving and they are more in the background, we will say for um, a lot of the beings, but they are very well connected to the spirit realm. And they are, they are wonderful teachers, and they are full of love energy. And they help guide and train the Yahyels, which should be next on your list. But they were, they were um, and they still are instrumental. They are like the spirit guides of the Yahyel and the teachers all wrapped up into one.

And the Yahyels! Woohoo! Teachers, they are not all Teachers, but they are very, very many who are, and they are dedicated to us. Even if they are not directly involved, like physically involved or mentally involved with us, they are still supporting us with their love energy. It is just an amazing race of beings. And they are the hybrids who did fit the bill, who will be coming and introduced to Earth and its inhabitants. And they will do a marvelous job. And those who are coming forth first are heroes! Because they understand the difficulties and the challenges of meeting a new race, of that Open Contact initial um encounters, because there are a lot of variables and we are playing the probabilities, trust us! But yes, that is a wonderful, wonderful thing, and they are wonderful, wonderful beings, and they are so focused. It is just like a love beam. If it hits you, you know it and you want more of it.

36:45 into the video

Leslie: You'll have to help me with the pronunciation of the next one, too. Sha'yana.

Hybrid Children: Again, please?

Leslie: Shay'la. Shay-lana? Shay'lana.

Hybrid Children: Sha'la'naya.

Leslie: Sha'la'naya. Thank you. Sha'la'naya.

Hybrid Children: Yes. That's us. That's us. It's just another fancy word for us. We are the First Ones. The first ones to come in to help humans to progress and evolve into the new future, which they have earned the right to participate in.

37:34 into the video

Leslie: En non? Anna Yaka?

Hybrid Children: Enannika?

Leslie: Very good. Thank you.

Hybrid Children: Yes, mindreading helps. Mindreading helps. Plus, we've seen the list. We're just waiting for you to struggle through it.

Leslie: I appreciate it.

Hybrid Children: More review would have been appropriate, Uncle Ray. But anyway, the Enannika are the next evolution of humans and the extraterrestrial races blending together. It is a new hybrid. And that hybrid species will be the culmination of the human race as you know it. As you believe that it exists. As it will have um, more of those vibratory qualities and abilities of humans which have been upgraded into a new, (pause) a new way of not only living, but a new way of loving, a new expansive way of connecting into the spirit realm and beyond. And that is the next evolution of Homo galacticus coming to rest into that word Enannika.

Leslie: Okay. Anu hay.

Hybrid Children: Anu'Het.

Leslie: Thank you.

    39:10 into the video

Hybrid Children: And sometimes when people say that, you want to say, "Oh, bless you. Did you sneeze?" But that is the combination, that is the ultimate conclusion of the hybrid races as far as this chapter of the universe and galactic family associations go. Because it will be a blending of all of the different hybrid races. We're going to pick out the best parts of all of them and combine them into one. And that is a thousand years into the humanity's future after Open Contact. And they will be a, the new non-physical race of humans. When humans reach the point where their vibrational level can no longer materialize except with con, with, with densifying a little bit. There will some that will still retain that ability. Not only, well, we will say for old time's sake, but they will be far beyond time at that time. But yes, that will be the ultimate conclusion of space-faring races for humanity, because they will escape to non-physicality and then they can come back and they can alter timelines and they can visit themselves as they were eons before. Not that they will want to do that. They won't be quite busy.

Leslie: What about counterparts?

Hybrid Children: Counter parts. Hmmmm.. We've seen counters. They have tops and they have bottoms. People put stuff on them, lots of stuff on them. Uncle Ray puts lots of stuff on them and leaves them there for a long time. So in some parts they're storage areas, but that's really not what you're talking about. The counterparts are generally conceived of as (sighs), and this is not an exact definition, as members of the same soul group. Because you guys really don't know what a soul group is. You say, "Oh, well, I'm from this soul group, and if they're from that soul group, then they must be a counterpart of mine." Well, in a literal sense, you can stretch that to be true. But in a practical sense, it doesn't work that way! Because you have so many different expressions from one particular soul group. And it's not really a soul group that you're coming from. It's just your soul. And your soul has lots of groupings which it chooses to explore. And not that the souls don't get together and hobnob and have their own little parties, but that is different.

41:58 into the video

Hybrid Children: But if there is a likeness or a connection between one soul group and another sometimes they get together, say, "Hey, why don't you invite your kids over to play with our kids?" and then that creates new forms of expression. And in that way, they become part of your soul group or your counterparts as well. So really it's anybody that you are connected with in a (pause) a more (pause) direct way, we will say is your counterpart. Because we are all One. But that is just a delineation which humans may use to understand some of the more obtuse concepts which you have come to try to understand and wrap your head around.

42:47 into the video

Leslie: Next, is Uncle Ray on the list.

Hybrid Children: Yayyyyy! Yayyyyy! Yayyyyy! Love being! Love being! Our microphone. He's our microphone. He's a sound system. We're connected. We're connected. We come through. We come through. And he has a future with usssss. He has a future with Open Contact! He has many different future roles. And he's going to have all kinds of people tugging at his sleeve and say, "What about this? What about this?" But he doesn't know about all that yet. Oh, and he's oh, he's an author. He's coming through with the books. And it is a non-stop process, because there are so many beings who are filling his head with new ideas and new processes and new structures for his new creations. And through that creativity, he will help lighten the world or enlighten the world in some ways. Yes. And that is an exciting subject for us. It is, it is, it hypes us up. And we don't even have to tug on his ego for that, because it…yeah, it's inflated enough as it is.

Leslie: (Laughs) How about timeline?

43:59 into the video

Hybrid Children: Timelines are (pause) innocuous descriptions of moment points. But humans think that they are physical things. Like kite strings and things like that, and they think, "Oh, well, there's a bunch of them close together." But it's more like a deck of a, a billion cards all being shuffled at the same time. And they get jumbled up, and they get mixed, and you choose from them all the time. You say, "Pick a card. Pick a card." That's kind of what you do with your reality to give it the illusion of linear unfoldment.

44:44 into the video

Leslie: Astral realm.

Hybrid Children: We're back to the mediumship again. Basically, the astral realm is a, is a storage unit of consciousness which have had experiences in physicality in the Earth realm. On the Earthen plane. And you can go, and you can check out people, or you can check out different forms of consciousness or events, because it's all stored there like some huge supercomputer. Electronically, of course. In your way of thinking. There's no outlets up there to plug into.

Leslie: Up there. Down there everywhere.

Hybrid Children: You've been there!

Leslie: (Laughs) Open invitation ET contact.

Hybrid Children: (Pause) Oh! Those, those are the parties that Uncle Ray holds.

Leslie: Yeah.

Hybrid Children: Yes. Yes. Those are very exciting. It is, it is a standing room only crowd which likes to come in. Because it is like the reverse of your um, um, circus attractions. And Ray is one of the circus attractions. Uncle Ray gets to sit there, and then all these beings get to come in like the, like in the fun house. And they get to come in. And they get to fly this ride, and then they get to talk about it a little bit to other beings like you. And they get to absorb all of that information. And unbeknownst to many of the attendees, they are actually interpreting and analyzing all of the responses of the attendees as well, because they can do that from an energetic level. Some of them can. And some of them communicate that to many other beings as well. So they can get multiple perspectives, and they can learn about more of that. Because the more beings and expressions of consciousness that other forms of consciousness learn about, the more creative they can be in expressing new novel forms of expansion which have never been thought of and created before. It is a service. It is a grouping. A big think tank we will say of exploration into Uncle Ray's head.

47:06 into the video

Leslie: Well, that's the end of Uncle Ray's list. If you have . . .

Hybrid Children: And the beginning of the story! And the beginning of the story! We are glad we got to say our piece. And though, although we said a lot of pieces. And we are grateful for your help and we will see how much of this makes it into the boooook, but it will be a fun project. It always is a fun project. And of course, we have never been known not to have fun because that's what we do. And although there are moments which are not as joyful as what we would like, we understand the need and the necessity for all of those expressions. Some of the other kinds of us who have already been on your planet have indeed experienced some hardships and some situations which we will not go into. But overall it is for the mission. That is the main focus. The Mission of Love. The mission of bringing more love to beings so that they can share more love. It is a, it is the greatest love story that your world has ever known! And you are all playing a part in it. And congratulations! You didn't even know that you auditioned! But you are all stars of love. Play on. Play on.

Leslie: Play on.

Hybrid Children: Okay. We don't need a lot of encouragement for that.

Leslie: Have fun.

Hybrid Children: And we will go. And let, and we can let Uncle Ray know and you can let Uncle Ray know that we could have done the names of the people who he left out because we love them all. They're all wonderful parts of High Vibe Channeling. So you can just put that down. That when they when he comes to their names or their groups, we can just put a line in there saying, "They are wonderful parts of High Vibe Channeling and loving and wonderful individuals and groups in their own right." So now we have answered all of those as well. And if there are any other things that he left out, welllll, he's just going to have to skip over them or call us back in, which would be fine. Which would be fine. Which would be fine. And we will goooo and we will thank you.

Leslie: Thank you!

Hybrid Children: Come and visit you in your dreams if you would like.

Leslie: Yes, please do

Hybrid Children: Ask us.

Leslie: Okay.

Hybrid Children: Ask us before sleep too, because it is a readiness thing, because at times, although that may be your input now at times you, your mind gets cloudy and you focus on other tangents because you have so many unanswered questions which come to you. It kind of sets the tone for your sleep parameters, we will say. But if you are joyful when you do that and you bring us in, and you are focused in that intent, it will happen.

Leslie: Thank you.

Hybrid Children: Thank you for understanding and thank you for your help and thank you for spreading the lovvvve. Woohoo!

Leslie: Thank you.

50:04 – They leave.

With apologies, the names and terms not given to the Hybrid Children in this session:

Aisling O'Donnell & Zariyah, Leslie Stewart & Orion, Heidi Slater & Diving Love Collective, Isabelle Rohach Zimmerman & Crystalline Love Collection, Dante Starshine Filipini & The Pleiadian Council.

"They are wonderful parts of High Vibe Channeling and loving and wonderful individuals and groups in their own right!"

Hybrid Children channeling by Ray Heitman 4/10/26

https://www.youtube.com/watch?v=0LjlqhoSNt8&t=1434s

www.ingramcontent.com/pod-product-compliance
Lightning Source LLC
Chambersburg PA
CBHW051821150726
47998CB00001B/242